The Feminine "No!"

SUNY series in Psychoanalysis and Culture

Henry Sussman, editor

The Feminine "No!"

Psychoanalysis and the
New Canon

Todd McGowan

STATE UNIVERSITY OF NEW YORK PRESS

Published by
State University of New York Press, Albany

© 2001 State University of New York

For information, address the State University of New York Press
90 State Street, Suite 700, Albany, NY 12207

Production by Kristin Milavec
Marketing by Anne M. Valentine

Library of Congress Cataloging-in-Publication Data

McGowan, Todd
    The feminine "no!" : psychoanalysis and the new canon / Todd McGowan.
      p. cm. — (SUNY series in psychoanalysis and culture)
    Includes bibliographical references and index.
    ISBN 0-7914-4873-8 (alk. paper)—ISBN 0-7914-4874-6 (pbk.)
    1. American fiction—History and criticism. 2. Psychological fiction, American—History
and criticism. 3. Gilman, Charlotte Perkins, 1860–1935. Yellow wall-paper. 4. Chopin,
Kate, 1851–1904. Awakening. 5. Chesnutt, Charles Waddell, 1858–1932. Marrow of
tradition. 6. Hurston, Zora Neale. Their eyes were watching God. 7. Psychoanalysis and
literature—United States—History. 8. Feminism and literature—United States—History. 9.
Canon (Literature). I. Title. II. Series.

PS374.P7 M37 2001
813.009'01'9—dc21   00-030079

10 9 8 7 6 5 4 3 2 1

For Mac Davis,
whose work made this possible

Contents

Acknowledgments

An earlier version of chapter 4, "Acting without the Father: Charles Chesnutt's New Aristocrat," appeared in *American Literary Realism, 1870–1910* 30.1 (Fall 1997): 59–74, and an earlier version of chapter 5, "Liberation and Domination: *Their Eyes Were Watching God* and the Evolution of Capitalism," appeared in *MELUS* 24.1 (Fall 1999).

I would like to thank those who helped this project along in its early stages, including George Hartley and the PLH, particularly Eleni Mavromatidou, Nathan Moore, and Ken Petri.

Thanks to Phil Foster, James Peltz, and Kristin Milavec, who helped the project through its later stages.

Thanks to Debra Moddelmog for her conscientious readings, and her continuing friendly counsel.

Thanks to Theresia de Vroom and Deborah Landeau for their many contributions, their being-toward-death, and their irony.

Finally, I owe the greatest debt to the three people without whom something could not have emerged out of nothing: Mac Davis, Paul Eisenstein, and Hilary Neroni.

1

The Canonical Unconscious

Many of the works that constitute today's new, revised canon of American literature have been the beneficiaries of rediscovery. The idea of rediscovery has been one of the principal motives behind the movement to change the canon, providing much of the impetus for this process. Rediscovery, of course, implies a prior loss. In other words, in order for the rediscovery of the works that constitute the new canon to be possible, they must, at some point, have been forgotten. And in order to understand the importance of their reemergence, it would seem to make sense that we must first have some idea of the reasons for this forgetting. If we understand why publishers, critics, and readers stopped (or never began) publishing, writing on, and reading these works, we should gain some purchase on what significance to attach to the fact that now they are published, written on, and read. The question is, then, Why were these works forgotten? According to Freud, we forget for one of three reasons: because what we perceive is unimportant and we are indifferent to it; because a perception is insufficiently different or distinct (so that it can be easily associated with an existing memory-trace); or because the perception was too traumatic and thus triggered resistance (resulting in repression).[1] Because all three of these types of forgetting have been at work in the formation of the canon of American literature, the canon-opening movement has worked, on different occasions, to counter each type. Thus, these distinctions can serve to guide our survey of the forgetting and subsequent rediscovery of literary works as it has occurred within the canon-opening movement.

Thinking about the exclusion of certain works from the canon as an act of "forgetting" involves deploying psychoanalytic concepts, developed

1

in reference to the individual subject's psyche, for the analysis of culture. There is, of course, ample precedent for this type of analysis in the Freudian oeuvre itself—*Totem and Taboo, Civilization and Its Discontents, Moses and Monotheism.* Even as he moves in this direction, however, Freud himself preaches caution: "I would not say that an attempt [. . .] to carry psycho-analysis over to the culture community was absurd or doomed to be fruitless. But we should have to be very cautious and not forget that, after all, we are only dealing with analogies and that it is dangerous, not only with men but also with concepts, to tear them from the sphere in which they have originated and been evolved."[2] Despite this disclaimer, Freud nonetheless (in the very book in which the disclaimer appears) both embarks upon and encourages the widening of the berth of psychoanalytic concepts to the cultural realm. He does this because he believes, in the last instance, that maintaining an absolute divide between the individual subject and the social order is untenable and implicitly posits a wholeness to the individual subject that it does not have. When we maintain a distinction between the individual and the collective, we ipso facto insist (as this way of putting it suggests) upon seeing the individual as self-identical and the collective divided, or as a conglomeration of many identities. For Freud, however, such a view subscribes to precisely the illusion of individual self-identity that psychoanalysis calls into question. Hence, in sustaining a divide between individual and collective, we partake of the illusion that the individual is not already a collective, not already a divided subject, the illusion that Freud was always at pains to shatter. If we think about it, it shouldn't be deploying psychoanalytic concepts in reference to the collective that we question, but more the use of them in reference to "individuals" about which we should raise doubts. This is especially true of the processes of forgetting, where we can see clear parallels between Freud's descriptions of forgetting on a psychical level and the forgetting that occurs in culture, in reference to the literary canon.

In the *Project for a Scientific Psychology,* Freud notes the importance of a pathway of facilitation for the memory of an impression to be possible. He says, "The memory of an experience (that is, its continuing operative power) depends on a factor which is called the magnitude of the impression and on the frequency with which the same impression is repeated."[3] Without a certain quantity of magnitude and frequency of repetition, we will not remember. We forget, in other words, because the impression fails to make much of an impression; it seems not to speak to us, and we react to it with indifference. Here, there is a parallel between individual and cultural forgetting, and we can draw the contours of this category in terms of literary works excluded from the canon. However, such works would not be, strictly speaking, literary. They would be works not considered worthy of literary study because they seemed so foreign to its field: works of science, of philosophy, of history, and even works that were literary but not "literary" enough, including journals, diaries, autobiographies, and so on. The traditional canon of American literature has forgotten—that is, not included—such works, and yet it is not possible to speak about repression in reference to their exclusion. They are forgotten precisely because, to use Freud's terms from the *Project,* there is no facilitation leading from them to other memory-traces within the canon, and this lack of facilitation makes it impossible for the impression of them to be retained. This is the forgetting that founds a symbolic entity—that is, the canon—through the constitution of an outside to that entity.[4] It is a necessary, initial forgetting that establishes a field, the gesture by which the literary canon exists at all in a meaningful way, by which there is something instead of nothing.

The attempt to recover this forgotten indifferent material has animated a significant part of the canon opening movement, because so much of the literary work done by excluded groups fits into this category. For instance, the slave narrative or autobiography was the predominant literary form for African Americans in the nineteenth century. To exclude this form from the very definition of "literary," to render it indifferent, would serve—and did serve—to de facto exclude African-American writing from the canon of nineteenth-century American literature. The journals of pre-nineteenth-century women provide a similar example, as does Native American oral literature. Many of the most well-known rediscoveries have been of this type: *The Narrative of the Life of Frederick Douglass, Incidents in the Life of a Slave Girl, A Narrative of the Captivity and Restoration of Mrs. Mary Rowlandson,* and *Black Elk Speaks* (just to name a few). When the editors of the third edition (1989) of the *Norton Anthology of American Literature* say they have made the anthology larger "to provide space for more *kinds* of American literature,"[5] they have in mind precisely the above-mentioned works. The kind of canon change that the emergence of such works represents is one that redefines the symbolic boundary indicated by the term "literature."[6] Canon opening has attacked the symbolic boundaries of the traditional canon in other significant ways as well, especially as part of a critique of the idea of purely aesthetic standards.

Much of the reconstruction of the literary canon that has taken place in recent years owes many of its successes to a critique of formalism in literary studies, a formalism that was instrumental in the formation of the canon of American literature.[7] This critique helped to expand the symbolic boundaries of the canon, to fight the forgetting that resulted from an arbitrary barrier separating the literary from the nonliterary. In breaking down this barrier, the critique of formalism exposed the political kernel lying within aesthetics; it made clear that there was no pure aesthetic judgment, that behind every aesthetic judgment was hidden a political one. For instance, Joyce Warren claims that "the mass exclusion of these 'other' writers from the canon of American literature is not simply a matter of aesthetic taste; it is also a political act."[8] The critique of formalism allows canon openers such as Warren to challenge the very idea of an aesthetic justification for the canonical status of literary texts. In fact, the idea of aesthetic excellence has fallen into such ill repute that few critics continue to invoke it at all.[9]

This fundamental insight—that the aesthetic is the political—opened up the possibility of a revaluation of the canon, because it called into question the ground of previous judgments of canonicity. Therefore, the once unimpeachable ground of masters like Nathaniel Hawthorne or William Faulkner lost some of its privileged aura (as did the work of art in Benjamin's famous essay), and the canon broadened. Just as no aesthetic judgment retained an aesthetic purity, neither did artistic creation retain its position transcendentally above culture. Criticism began to see the artist less as creator and more as cultural product. Grasping this trend, Cecelia Tichi, in her overview of New Historicism, notes that "to call Melville a genius or great author is emphatically to remove him from his cultural milieu."[10] This undercutting of privileged ground created a space for writers, such as Lydia Maria Child or Fanny Fern, perceived to be of cultural or political—rather than aesthetic—significance, to rise in importance, just as it demonstrated the culture and political aspects of the "masters."[11] Hence, it allowed the canon to include a broad range of works that the traditional canon could not but regard as indifferent material. The indifferent, however, though it can involve repression, is not the repressed. The recovery of these works, while clearly important, is thus not the return of the repressed, simply because of their difference. To remember them is to access new memory facilitations, but not the overloaded facilitations that have been isolated as a result of repression.

The second category of forgetting includes, in complete contrast to the first, that which is too easily assimilable. These impressions are not indifferent, and they do not lack facilitations. Their pathway, on the contrary, is all too facilitated. They are so similar to existing memory-traces with which they associate (through the process of facilitation) that they produce no memory-trace of their own. In other words, this is the kind of forgetting that occurs when everything blurs together and when it is impossible to separate the memory of one thing from the memory of another. As Freud says in *The Psychopathology of Everyday Life,* such memory-traces "succumb unresistingly to the process of condensation."[12] As such, they are cases of what Freud calls "the *normal* process of forgetting."[13] In terms of contemporary literature, these are the books of Tom Clancy and Danielle Steele, books that can so readily be assimilated to other books in the genre that they are indistinct. In the history of American literature, we can see this kind of forgetting in the exclusion from the canon of works like Susan Warner's *Wide, Wide World* and Zane Grey's *Riders of the Purple Sage.*

This kind of forgetting has been of great importance to a historicist approach, which seeks the conscious essence of a historical or cultural epoch—what such an epoch thinks about itself. Jane Tompkins was one of those at the fore of this movement, which has today, in the forms of new historicism and cultural studies, become predominant. In *Sensational Designs* (an explicit attempt at canon opening), Tompkins argues for a change in the very concept of what constitutes literature and its study, and in what makes a literary work worthy of study. According to her, "novels and stories should be studied not because they manage to escape the limitations of their particular time and place, but because they offer powerful examples of the way a culture thinks about itself, articulating and proposing solutions for the problems that shape a particular historical moment."[14] If the authors that Tompkins rediscovers—Susan Warner, Harriet Beecher Stowe, Charles Brockden Brown, and others—are easily assimilated to other memory-traces, then all the better, because what we should seek in canonical literature is precisely the well-facilitated memory path. As Tompkins points out, "I have not tried to emphasize the individuality of genius of the authors in question, to isolate the sensibility, modes of perception, or formal techniques that differentiate them from other authors or from one another. Rather, I have seen them, in Foucault's phrase, as 'nodes within a network,' expressing what lay in the minds of many or most of their contemporaries."[15]

Certainly, the recovery of what has been forgotten in this way has its importance: it does provide insight into the consciousness of prior historical epochs. This importance, however, is limited, because in rediscovering "what lay in the minds" of a particular culture at a particular moment in this way, we restrict ourselves primarily to consciousness and ignore the unconscious. In such works, we tend to see what an epoch wants to think about itself, not what it doesn't. The very popularity of a work such as Stowe's *Uncle Tom's Cabin* suggests that what it had to say was something that people wanted to hear and that it allowed people to see themselves in the way in which they wanted to be seen. When we rediscover such popular works and thus find out the conscious mind of the epoch, we don't touch on the unconscious.[16] Material that has been forgotten because it is too common is never unconscious material in the dynamic sense (i.e., repressed material). What the rediscovery of it fails to give us is any indication of the truth of the canon itself—that is, what the canon absolutely cannot admit and must repress.

Thus, we come to the third category of forgetting—repression. Repression is a forgetting that emerges in response to an impression that overloads the psychical apparatus. This overload has effects in the psyche, as Freud says in the *Project,* "as though there had been a stroke of lightning."[17] It tears down the barriers set up within the psychic system, leaving "permanent facilitations behind [...] which possibly do away with the resistance of the contact-barrier entirely and establish a pathway of conduction."[18] The barriers that protect the psyche—its defenses— lose their effectiveness in the aftermath of an overload of excitation. In response to this traumatic overload, the psyche represses, which involves keeping the impression as far from consciousness as possible. As Freud puts in his essay on "Repression," *"the essence of repression lies simply in turning something away, and keeping it at a distance, from the conscious."*[19] Repression does not, however, eliminate memory-traces of the impression from the unconscious, but in fact works to constitute the unconscious proper. If forgetting has been tendentious and we may rightly call it a repression, then the works that fit into this category of forgetting are the unconscious of the canon, and as such, they have a truth to tell us— nothing less than the truth of the canon itself—because, as Freud tell us in *The Interpretation of Dreams,* "the unconscious is the true psychical reality."[20]

Which leaves us with an important question: How do we distinguish repression from the first two categories of forgetting? Perhaps we can find the answer in the nature of repression itself. Repression, unlike other forgetting, is not something done once and then completed. It must be constantly sustained, and it must be sustained extra-symbolically. Freud points out that "the process of repression is not to be regarded as an event which takes place *once,* the results of which are permanent, as when some living thing has been killed and from that time onward is dead; repression demands a persistent expenditure of force."[21] What has been repressed continues to haunt us, refusing to die once and for all, and necessitating "force" rather than symbolic activity to be forgotten. In terms of the canon, this means that the canon's repressed does not include those works that can be dismissed conclusively on the basis of a set of—however arbitrarily constructed—canonical criteria (such as aesthetic considerations, etc.). When canonical criteria form the basis for an exclusion from the canon, this indicates a symbolic exclusion, but not a repression. A work repressed by the traditional canon must *not* have been excluded because of aesthetic deficiencies, because of a failure to meet certain formal standards, but must have necessitated a show of force. In other words, this kind of exclusion is an irrational forgetting, one not following from the formal standards that guide all the other exclusions (and inclusions).

For many years, formalist demands, often of a New Critical variety, were the theoretical justification for decisions about the value of literary works and their place within the canon.[22] These criteria (complexity, ambiguity, irony—in short, difficulty) readily account for the exclusion of certain works, such as, for instance, Lydia Maria Child's *Hobomok,* a novel that makes no bones about its political aims. But this act of forgetting is not a repression precisely because it has a once-and-for-all quality to it and because it works symbolically. Once the formalist criteria are in place, there is no need to give another thought to a work like *Hobomok.* It doesn't trouble the sleep of our formalist critic, because this exclusion makes sense within the formalist symbolic system. If something can be symbolically explained—made sense of within a particular symbolic system—then it does not require an act of repression. Repression only becomes necessary when the symbolic system does not facilitate the exclusion of something that must nevertheless be excluded.

We encounter repression when we discover those works whose exclusion from the canon doesn't make sense, is *non-sensical.* In other words, what about those excluded works that, according to even New Critical criteria, should be canonical mainstays? These are the works that strain a system of symbolization, which for the symbolic entity we call the traditional canon occupy an unsymbolizable place—the place of what Lacan calls the Real. For many involved with canon opening, canon exclusion is exclusively a symbolic business, and hence demands a symbolic revolution: old standards excluded works by marginalized writers, new standards must be inclusive of these works. This project has its value—it has made possible access to the repressed of the canon—but because it remains wholly within symbolic considerations and doesn't consider the failure of the symbolic, it doesn't touch on the Real. It is precisely this Real that the pages that follow will attempt to engage, which is why the works under discussion will not be those whose exclusion from the canon formalist criticism can explain, but those whose exclusion it can't. These exclusions take us by surprise, and in this lies their importance. This is why Freud says in *The Psychopathology of Every-day Life* that "I am as a rule only concerned with [. . .] those [cases] in which the forgetting *surprises* me because I should have expected to know the thing in question."[23] Certain exclusions take us by surprise precisely because, according to the prevailing criteria, they should be included in the canon. These works—and I will discuss four: Charlotte Perkins Gilman's "The Yellow Wall-paper," Kate Chopin's *The Awaken-ing*, Charles Chesnutt's *The Marrow of Tradition*, and Zora Neale Hurston's *Their Eyes Were Watching God*—because of the senselessness of their exclusion, because, in a word, of their repression, represent our path to the canonical unconscious.[24]

The term "canonical unconscious" necessarily implies the existence of an unconscious on a cultural level, what seems like the Jungian "collective unconscious." According to Freud, however, Jung's term is misleading, and it is misleading for two very different reasons: it implies the existence of a collective soul that unites humanity, and, even more important, it leads us to believe (incorrectly) that the unconscious can ever be anything but collective. As Freud says in *Moses and Monotheism*, "I do not think that much is to be gained by introducing the concept of a 'collective' unconscious—the content of the unconscious is collective anyhow, a general possession of mankind."[25] The unconscious is always "collective anyhow" because it exists in reference to the symbolic function, at the point of the symbolic order's failure. Although the content of the unconscious varies for different subjects, it nonetheless exists in the same place vis-à-vis the symbolic order—that is, in the place of the unsymbolizable. This becomes clear in Lacan's echo of Freud's refusal of the term "collective unconscious." He asks, "What solution could seriously be expected from the word 'collective' in this instance, when the collective and the individual are strictly the same thing? No, it isn't a matter of positing a communal soul somewhere, [. . .] it isn't a question of psychological entification, it is a question of the symbolic function."[26] In other words, the unconscious is structural, rather than substantial, and it exists in reference to the symbolic order. It always exists at the same place—a gap in the symbolic chain—which is why we can talk about it in cultural terms, though the pathway to this place is clearly subject to individual variation.

If we grasp the structural nature of the unconscious—that it is always in the same place—then we can see that it makes little difference whether we are talking about the unconscious of an individual or that of a culture. In both cases, the term "unconscious" refers to that position within the symbolic order where symbolization breaks down. It is in this sense as well that the unconscious is not historical, not subject to the variegations of historical change. At every point in history, what cannot be spoken is the symbolic order's failure, because if it is spoken, it is no longer a failure, precisely because it is spoken. That is, to speak the failure of the symbolic order is already to *not* speak that failure, to attest to that order's success rather than its failure. The point at which the symbolic order fails is always a traumatic point, because when we arrive there we can't find the words to make sense of it. It remains nonsensical—as with the forgetting of the four works under discussion here—creating a quantity of excitation that cannot be discharged and thereby blocking the normal pathways of the memory. This is the process of repression.

For decades, these works went unremarked on by critics, untaught by teachers, and unpublished by presses. And yet, judged by their formal qualities alone, they would seem to be among the great works of American literature. We can see one piece of evidence for this in the sheer number of critical disputes these works have engendered since their recovery, disputes not about inclusion or exclusion, but about interpretive difficulties. For formalist criticism, aesthetic excellence begets a kind of critical fecundity: the greater a work of literature is, the more criticism it gives rise to (because of its ambiguity and difficulty, two of the fundamental values of this criticism). This kind of formalist aesthetic thus determines aesthetic value by the richness of the literary work, by the amount of material a work provides for interpretation. According to this standard, "The Yellow Wall-paper," *The Awakening, The Marrow of Tradition,* and *Their Eyes Were Watching God* have shown themselves to be some of the richest works in American literature, each occasioning a myriad of critical debates since their recovery. This richness suggests to us that the exclusion of these four works was an act of repression, because in all ways they fit the criteria for the canon.

But the most important indication that a repression has taken place is the presence of a trauma. We repress only what is traumatic—an impression that the psyche (or in this case the canon) cannot handle. At this point, then, the next logical step would thus seem to be an inquiry into the response that these four works engendered at their initial publication and then concluding from this response why they were never acknowledged canonically. Such a historicist approach might recount, for instance, the words of Horace Scudder (the editor at *Atlantic Monthly*), noted by Charlotte Perkins Gilman in *The Living of Charlotte Perkins Gilman,* when he, after reading it with horror, rejected "The Yellow

Wall-paper" for publication: "I could not forgive myself if I made others as miserable as I have made myself!"[27] Or, it could recount the shock of William Dean Howells (until then, a staunch supporter of Charles Chesnutt) on reading Chesnutt's *The Marrow of Tradition,* a novel that Howells claimed "would be better if it was not so bitter."[28] Such responses, though they may be exemplary, cannot, however, indicate the presence of a trauma, precisely because they are (symbolic) articulations of why these works are objectionable made contemporaneously with their repression. One cannot name a trauma or repressed material *while it remains traumatic and repressed*—such is the very nature of repression. Reasons for a repression may be given at the time of the repression, but if a repression is at work, these will never be *the* reasons for the repression. The trauma itself, at the time of repression, cannot be named, because repression removes material from consciousness. If someone could have said, at the time, precisely what was traumatic about these works, there would have been no need for repression. The articulation of the trauma does away with the repression of the trauma, as Breuer discovers, much to his surprise, during his treatment of Anna O. The fact that "each symptom disappeared after she had described its first occurrence" reveals to Breuer the relationship between symbolization and trauma: if we are able to symbolize a trauma, it ceases to be a trauma, and the symptom that it has produced disappears.[29] Whatever contemporaries said about the traumatic dangers of these four works, these words— because they are words and because they were spoken when they were spoken—cannot help us.

It is only in hindsight, after the trauma has ceased to be traumatic, that it can speak. This is why the historicist approach is doomed to miss the repressed: it can only discover conscious reasons for forgetting or exclusion, not unconscious ones. At the time of its repression, the repressed *could not speak* in a way that made sense—and it could not be spoken about. In digging up what was actually said historically about these works, we can never find—no matter how exhaustive our research— a direct word on the repressed itself, simply because such a word cannot exist. The reasons editors, critics, and readers gave—if they gave reasons at all—were reasons that had nothing to do with the repression, but served as a screen for it. After the repressed has returned, however, we can begin to hear what it would have said when no one could have heard it. When the repressed returns, it starts to speak for the first time. This is why Lacan says, in *Seminar I,* that "repression and the return of the repressed are the same thing."[30] The return allows us to hear retroactively what the repressed had to say in the past. Only through listening for the return of the repressed through interpretation can the past act of repression be discovered. This is why psychoanalysis necessarily focuses on forging a *construction* of the primal, traumatic scene, rather than trying to access a memory of it. The original scene is only traumatic retroactively, in the future anterior—it will have been traumatic. In other words, only after the fact can we construct the scene that necessitated the repression, as is most clearly illustrated in Freud's analysis of the Wolf Man. For Freud, whether or not the Wolf Man really witnessed the primal scene suggested by his dream of wolves in a tree is wholly beside the point, because such a scene is inevitably a construction. As Freud puts it, "Scenes from infancy are not reproduced during the treatment as recollections, they are the products of construction."[31] Hence, only as a construction after the fact, only when the repressed returns, can we discover what was traumatic about "The Yellow Wall-paper," *The Awakening, The Marrow of Tradition,* and *Their Eyes Were Watching God,* now that they aren't traumatic any longer. And when we recognize the presence of trauma—where the trauma was—we gain insight into why these works were repressed.

The difficulty of achieving such insight stems from the nonsensical nature of repression. The act of repression doesn't make sense because it isn't a symbolic act. Though symbolic justifications by and large successfully sustained a relatively homogeneous canon, some works, because the symbolic justification could not work for them, demanded an extra-symbolic act of repression, an act of force. Today, however, as these works have made their way into the canon, the repressed has returned, seemingly opening up this canonical unconscious. They are no longer excluded and have become part of a new canonical symbolic structure. The effect of this inclusion is not, as we might expect, a breakthrough revelation of a heretofore repressed unconscious. It is, instead, a closing up of that unconscious. Contrary to what we might expect, the traumatic kernel of these works—what provoked their repression—is not now, all of a sudden, revealed. Instead, the trauma is even further repressed. When these works were excluded from the old canon, the unconscious was open, but it remained inaccessible precisely because no one could read the works that would reveal it. When they were included in the new canon, this was, as Lacan says in *Seminar XI,* "a making present of the closure of the unconscious" and an "enactment of the reality of the unconscious."[32] At the moment at which the unconscious is realized and thus made accessible to interpretation, it closes up, precisely because it ceases to be unconscious. But while the unconscious is open, it remains inaccessible to interpretation. This is the bind we face when approaching the unconscious. The more that the canonical repressed gets symbolized, the less truth it has to tell us. And increasing symbolization has been the driving force behind the canon opening movement.[33] This increasing symbolization makes it almost impossible to see what was ever traumatic about these works in the first place. We rightly wonder, if they were so traumatic, why is everyone so eager to publish them, read them, and write about them today?

The emergence of formerly marginalized texts into the literary canon represents a fundamental change in some aspects of the controlling logic of that canon—a change toward a wider symbolization. As Paul Lauter explains in his discussion of canon change, "the major issue is not assimilating some long-forgotten works or authors into the existing categories; rather, it is reconstructing historical understanding to make it inclusive and explanatory instead of narrowing and arbitrary."[34] In a pamphlet advertising a new edition of *The Heath Anthology of American Literature,* the anthology on the forefront of canon change, its editors claim that it "represents a reconception of the very nature of literature in America."[35] These new visions of the canon see it as, for one, nonhomogeneous; that is, the canon no longer tells—and American literature is no longer conceived as—an uninterrupted narrative of literary evolution. It is now clear that this historical evolution has been marked by wide cultural divergence also. For instance, Arnold Krupat points out that much of Native American literature, unlike most white American literature, "attempt[s] to present many voices in [one] text [which] has the result of legitimating those voices."[36] Hence, because they create meaning in a way unlike works already in the canon, the introduction of such texts into the canon of American literature demands a shift in its logic—a shift to a logic of inclusion (i.e., increasing symbolization).[37] Canon changes have been possible because new texts have been admitted under the principle of inclusion—and "inclusion" has become the watchword of canon change. The 1989 (third) edition of *The Norton Anthology of American Literature,* the most popular literary anthology, had to undergo a physical change in the volume in order to make room for new writers. In their discussion of the writers added to their canon (which is, clearly, what this anthology is meant to approximate), the editors claim that the "new authors expand and enrich" the volume, thus demonstrating, in their praise of the anthology, inclusion—and symbolization—of difference as the driving force behind their work.

Over the last three decades (but beginning in earnest in the late 1980s), this process of symbolization has proceeded, as the former canonical repressed has taken a place at the center of the new canon. The movement for the rediscovery of forgotten works had its genesis in the late 1960s and early 1970s. We can see the contours of this movement most prominently in publishing history. Prior to that time, what are now considered major works in the American literary canon were out of print—and had been so for decades. As late as 1963, "The Yellow Wall-paper," *The Awakening, The Marrow of Tradition,* and *Their Eyes Were Watching God* were all out of print. In addition, all of the other works of Charlotte Perkins Gilman, Kate Chopin, Charles Chesnutt, and Zora Neale Hurston were also out of print. Just over thirty-five years ago, these four writers, who today are central canonical figures, were not even considered important enough to have *one* book in print among all of them. Between 1964 and 1974, all of the above-mentioned works came back into print. Putnam first published *The Awakening* in 1964; Gregg, Arno, and the University of Michigan all published *The Marrow of Tradition* in 1969; Fawcett World published *Their Eyes Were Watching God* in 1969; the Feminist Press published "The Yellow Wall-paper" in 1974. Some additional small presses began to publish these works in the following years, and then, in the mid-1980s and after, the major presses began to take an interest in them.

As of 1996, there were *twenty-two* editions of *The Awakening* in print, including those of Random House, Norton, McGraw-Hill, Knopf, Bantam, and Penguin (not exactly marginalized presses). The popularity of this novel in particular has increased so dramatically that it would be silly to continue to call it a "noncanonical" work; it has become part of the core of the nineteenth-century American literary canon. This represents an incredible shift from its status in 1963: out of print and almost completely ignored. Other changes have been perhaps less dramatic, but still quite apparent. In 1993, Penguin published a "Penguin Classics" edition of Chesnutt's *The Marrow of Tradition.* It also appeared in Dutton's 1992 *The African-American Novel in the Age of Reaction: Three Classics,* and Vintage's *Three Classic African-American Novels.* The emergence of these editions reveal Chesnutt's increasing importance as a canonical figure. The new editions of most of Zora Neale Hurston's work (her four novels, two books on folklore, and autobiography) published in 1990 by HarperCollins reveal much the same thing. Gilman's "The Yellow Wall-paper" is now in print in seven editions (including a Bantam edition) and in the 1992 *Charlotte Perkins Gilman Reader.*[38] All four writers now also have a significant presence in current literary anthologies.

The presence of a work in a literary anthology is at the same time a sign of and an argument for its canonicity. That is, the anthology both represents the contemporary canon and helps to form it. This latter, more active aspect, is not now openly avowed by the anthologies themselves, though it was in the past.[39] In the preface to the 1970 edition of Houghton Mifflin's *American Poetry and Prose,* the editors proclaimed, "*American Poetry and Prose* has helped to shape and inform the changing canon of our literature since publication of the first edition in 1925. It is our belief that it will continue to do so for the critical generation of students coming of age in the 1970's."[40] Though they continue to function in this active way, contemporary anthologies tend to stress only their role in "representing" the canon, rather than in creating and substantiating it. Nevertheless, the presence of a work in an anthology is an indicator, as much as its publication history, of its status in regard to the canon, especially after the explosion in popularity of anthologies in the 1980s. The publication of the first edition of the *Norton Anthology of American Literature* in 1979 dramatically changed the face of literary studies, especially in college classrooms. It made many works—even complete novels—available in an accessible and handy form. The success of the *Norton* format can be measured simply by noting the emergence of several similar anthologies in its wake. The presence or nonpresence of a work in the *Norton Anthology* thus became more and more a significant factor in a work's canonical status, as the anthology's popularity grew. In the first edition of 1979, no works from Charlotte Perkins Gilman, Charles Chesnutt, or Zora Neale Hurston appeared in the *Norton Anthology.* Kate Chopin's *The Awakening* did appear, as part of the anthology's attempt to redress critical neglect of women writers. In the second edition of 1985, however, "The Yellow Wall-paper" and one story by both Chesnutt and Hurston appear, and *The Awakening* is no longer presented as an example of the anthology's breadth of coverage, but is included without comment, accepted as a fully legitimized part of the canon.

The full canonization of major rediscovered figures such as Gilman, Chesnutt, Chopin, and Hurston occurs in the 1989 edition of the anthology. In this third edition, all of these writers have become staples of the anthology and accepted members of the canon it professes to represent, and they no longer garner any special mention as significant recent additions. In fact, the language of the preface undergoes a notable evolution from the 1985 edition. In the earlier (1985) edition, the editors claimed,

> A major responsibility of this Norton Anthology is to redress the long neglect of woman writers in America. In the new edition,

almost eight hundred pages represent the work of thirty-five women (six more than in the first edition), from Davis to Walker. Another responsibility is to do justice to the contributions of black writers to American literature and culture; we include sixteen black authors who provide the opportunity to trace explicit discussions of the distinctly black experience in both polemical and imaginative writings.[41]

The language that suggests an ethical responsibility (redressing neglect and doing justice) disappears in the 1989 edition, and the emphasis turns to expansion and greater inclusion.[42] This is significant because it clearly indicates a change in attitude: the inclusion of white women writers and African-American writers is not something exceptional that needs justifying in ethical terms. Equal "representation" has become the norm. This change in attitude in the *Norton Anthology,* one of the more conservative and traditional anthologies, leaves little doubt that a radical transformation has taken place.[43]

Changes in the *Norton Anthology,* given its groundbreaking presence and its centrality in American Literature classrooms, illustrate the movement of the foundation of the canon, but it is *The Heath Anthology,* an anthology expressly created with concerns of multiculturalism in mind, which shows the real forward movement of canon change. The first edition of *The Heath Anthology* appeared in 1989, and its success prompted a second edition in 1993. Selections from Gilman, Chopin, Chesnutt, and Hurston all appear in the first edition, which is not surprising, given the motives working in the creation of this anthology. Its project, according to an advertising pamphlet, is "a reconception of the very nature of literature in America," an attempt to reconceive the canon in light of rediscoveries of heretofore "lost" writers and also a shifting emphasis in the values by which literary works are judged.[44] In light of this attempt, the creators of *The Heath Anthology* claim that "it is the truest picture available of our literature—the *real* American literature."[45] The basis for this claim clearly lies in the breadth of the anthology's symbolization, in its "project to reconstruct American literature" based on the idea of inclusion.[46]

The third indicator of a changing literary climate (after print histories and anthologies) is the volume of criticism written about literary works. The number of critical articles and books written about a work indicates, probably more directly than a print history or presence in an anthology, the estimate of a work in the academy at large. Of the three, this is the area less directly influenced by market factors, the will of publishers, and so forth. In 1960, according to the *MLA International Bibliography,* there were no works of criticism written about Gilman, Chopin, or Chesnutt, and one brief article written on Hurston. In 1990, there were eleven works on Gilman, thirteen on Chopin, five on Chesnutt, and seventeen on Hurston. Clearly, over this thirty-year period a dramatic change has taken place. It is also evident if we look at larger spans of time. Throughout the entire decade of the 1960s (and despite the fact that the recovery of Chesnutt and Chopin was already well underway),[47] there were no works of criticism written on Gilman, twelve on Chesnutt (including many introductions to republished editions of his books), eight on Chopin, and two on Hurston. The first *half* of the 1990s reveals a remarkably different climate: fifty-six works on Gilman, twenty-three on Chesnutt, one-hundred and thirty on Chopin, and one-hundred and forty-two on Hurston. This trend illustrates that the rediscoveries of these writers have been internalized by the academy, that they have become very much a part of what critics write about. The shift indicates most forcefully that these writers are no longer a part of the canonical repressed.

Through this massive effort to remember the repressed, what is necessarily missed is what the repressed reveals—its truth. The very act of remembering indicates a closing up of the unconscious. We can understand this through a reference to remembering dreams. For Freud, a dream offers us our unconscious desire, albeit in a disguised form. But there are, we might say, two different types of dreams—those we can remember and those we can't. In the latter, the dream-work (or, the functioning of symbolization) does not succeed in disguising a trauma well enough so that we can become conscious of it, whereas in the former, the disguise is effective in diffusing the trauma. In these two types of dreams, we should see a distinction between symbolization and repression. The "effective" dream offers us the real through, for instance, displacement or condensation: in a dream, my mother appears in the guise of my spouse. I can easily recount the dream, because it situates a trauma in a symbolic form. It is not necessarily the content of the displacement—spouse for mother—that diffuses the trauma, but the very form of the dream itself. Here, the dream parallels symbolization precisely: both function primarily not to disguise reality but to provide respite from a trauma or a threat.

Some dreams, however, even though they are symbolic by virtue of their form, nonetheless take us to an encounter with trauma, albeit through the mechanism of the symbol.[48] These are the dreams we are not all that eager to remember in the morning—so we repress. Like symbolization, repression also provides a respite, but of a fundamentally different order, because the threat repressed is such that it cannot be revealed, even through the mechanism of the symbol. With repression, I do not simply remember the dream in a distorted form, but I don't remember it at all. This indicates a threat or a trauma such that it can't be symbolized away, which is why both Freud and Lacan place such importance on what a patient forgets. In forgetting lies the key to trauma. In his *Seminar I,* Lacan suggests that "the most significant dream would be the dream that has been completely forgotten, one about which the subject couldn't say anything."[49] Where there is repression, there is a threat so dangerous that it cannot be spoken or recounted. When nothing is forgotten, however, this indicates that the threat has been symbolized, that repression is no longer necessary. This is precisely the process that Freud describes the ego orchestrating in the *Project:* the ego subdues the intensity of the trauma through what Freud calls "side-cathexes," or what we might see as connections to signifiers. He says,

> If the trauma (experience of pain) occurs—the very first [trau-mas] escape the ego altogether—at a time when there is already an ego, there is to begin with a release of unpleasure, but simul-taneously the ego is at work too, creating side-cathexes. If the cathexis of the memory is repeated, the unpleasure is repeated too, but the ego-facilitations are there already as well; experience shows that the release [of unpleasure] is less the second time, until, after further repetition, it shrivels up to the intensity of a signal acceptable to the ego.[50]

Through the process of symbolization (linking the trauma up with more and more signifiers or pathways of facilitation), we do away with the need for continued repression. This end of repression means that the unconscious no longer speaks, that where it was once open, it is now closed. When the trauma can be symbolized, it no longer remains a trauma, and it no longer speaks the truth of our being. It is this end of a trauma—this closing of the unconscious—that we can see in the can-onization of "The Yellow Wall-paper," *The Awakening, The Marrow of Tradition,* and *Their Eyes Were Watching God.* Today, these works no longer dwell in obscurity, but proliferate on course syllabi, as dissertation subjects, and amid publisher's catalogues. The more they proliferate, the less they speak qua unconscious, simply because symbolization always silences the unconscious, closes it up.

　　That said, it would be disingenuous to lament the closing up of the unconscious, because without its closing we never have access to it. If the unconscious did not close, the four works we are discussing wouldn't be in print or available for discussion at all. But as we move further and further away from the moment of this closing—the moment of the rediscovery of these works—we risk losing sight of the opening altogether, obscuring the fact that these works were once traumatic, though they no longer are. We risk, to put it in pseudo-Heideggerian terms, forgetting the earlier forgetting. The more that we symbolize these works (publish them, read them, write about them—in short, canonize them), the less it becomes imaginable that they were ever traumatic, and they become so commonplace that whatever edge they once had becomes thoroughly dulled. Soon, they come to seem just like other works written at the time, part of a historical continuity, rather than a disruption of it. This process has occurred with each of the four works under discussion here. Where once critics saw disruption, today they see continuity. Where once they saw the Real, today they see a symbolic chain. Before getting to the individual examples of this process, however, we should first look at the moments through which, as a rule, all traumatic discoveries move.

The discovery—or rediscovery—of something traumatic typically moves through three different moments: they are, according to Lacan, the instant of the glance, the time for comprehending, and the moment for concluding.[51] First, in the instant of the glance, the traumatic discovery appears as a purely contingent happening: we know that what we have uncovered is important, but we don't know or fail to see where that importance lies. At this point, in other words, we know only that the material is traumatic, but not why it's traumatic—or how it changes anything. Here, discovery has the status of the Real. This is why the initial discoverer is always blind to her or his own discovery: the brightness of the point of discovery makes it impossible to discern the discovery's impact. Second, in the time for comprehending, after we become thoroughly familiar with the traumatic material, it loses its traumatic edge and becomes indistinguishable from the rest of the symbolic network in which it is embedded. The traumatic Real of the initial discovery gets symbolized, integrated into an already existing narrative structure. Here, we actually become overacquainted with the discovery, thereby allowing it to become common sense—something everyone recognizes and thus something that can't possibly be traumatic. Our familiarity becomes a barrier to knowing the importance of the discovery, to recognizing the trauma.[52] Third, however, in the moment for concluding, we are able to see the trauma once again, but this time we can understand it, grasp its significance, because it is no longer traumatic. Like the initial response, the third moment also sees something traumatic in the material, though it also sees that trauma within a symbolic locus.[53] At this point, we are able to see precisely how the traumatic discovery represents something new. In this sense, the moment for concluding owes a debt to the time for comprehending because the way in which it obscures the trauma can point us in the direction of that trauma's significance. Even more important, the time for comprehending also provides distance from the trauma through its symbolization, and this distance offers us room to make sense of it. By dimming the initial brightness of the traumatic discovery, the time for comprehending allows us to look at it without being blinded, so that we can grasp its significance.

We can see a concrete example of this process in, of all places, Freud's discovery of psychoanalysis and the unconscious. Initially, of course, this discovery had a definite traumatic edge, undercutting the priority of consciousness (and its supposed self-transparency) in the human subject. Freud's comment to Jung as they were arriving in America—"They don't realize we're bringing them the plague"—indicates that he himself was well aware of the traumatic import of his discovery. Instead of being a "plague" to America, however, it would be more accurate to say that the plague worked in the other direction. American-centered ego psychology managed to dull the traumatic edge of Freud's discovery, rendering it palatable, not so plague-like. In this way, psychoanalysis lost its radical edge and became a vehicle for normalization. It was in response to this situation that Jacques Lacan authored his "return to Freud," which aimed at restoring the traumatic dimension of the Freudian discovery by emphasizing the way in which that discovery involved a complete rethinking of subjectivity. In this way, Lacan returned the difficulty to Freud and at the same time made clear precisely where the trauma of the Freudian discovery lay.

Lacan repeats the Freudian discovery, and this repetition isolates its original trauma. For Lacan, the traumatic importance of the discovery lies in its displacement of the ego from the center of the subject, its rejection of the priority of the ego. Not coincidentally, Lacan latches on to the dimension of Freudian thought that ego psychology explicitly downplays and minimizes. Emphasizing the structural model of the psyche that Freud developed in the 1920s, ego psychology pictures analysis as a process of allowing the ego to "regain" the upper hand over the unconscious. Buttressing and strengthening the ego become, in this therapeutic universe, the most important contributions of psychoanalysis. Thus, ego psychology strips psychoanalysis of its danger, its traumatic force, and works to normalize it (just as it works to normalize subjects in therapy). Nonetheless, the very focus of this normalization—what ego

psychology chooses to emphasize (the ego) and deemphasize (the unconscious)—paves the way for the Lacanian return to Freud. In response
to the obfuscations of ego psychology, Lacan grasps just what it was
about Freud's discovery that was traumatic—its displacement of the ego
and its grasp of the split in the subject.[54] Ego psychology, though it does
its best to efface the traumatic impact of the discovery of psychoanalysis,
ends up making it possible for Lacan to identify the significance of that
traumatic impact, to locate it in its specificity. Through this example, we
can see precisely how the time for comprehending (the obscuring of its
traumatic impact) is crucial for the moment for concluding (which grasps
the meaning of the trauma).

Discoveries have to occur twice, and they must do so for two reasons. First, after an initial discovery, there necessarily occurs a period in
which that discovery becomes normalized and symbolized, in which its
importance is lost. Second, when a discovery first makes itself felt, it
appears as a contingent occurrence—as an irruption of the Real—and it
is impossible to grasp where, precisely, the significance of the discovery
lies. This is why Hegel insists, in the *Philosophy of History,* that all revolutions must occur twice. He says, "In all periods of the world a political
revolution is sanctioned in men's opinions, when it repeats itself. Thus
Napoleon was twice defeated, and the Bourbons twice expelled. By repetition that which at first appeared merely a matter of chance and contingency, becomes a real and ratified existence."[55] To put it in Lacanian
terms, in its first manifestation we perceive a revolution as Real, then we
symbolize it (thereby obscuring its radicality), and finally we see the way
in which it has effected a fundamental change upon symbolic relations
(that it has not simply been assimilated). We can see a similar trajectory
in the critical history of the four rediscovered works under discussion
here, except that in each case we remain at the stage of symbolization,
in which critics are intent on denying the traumatic edge of these works
and are determined to demonstrate their continuity with the prevailing
symbolic network.

When readers and critics first rediscovered these works, they greeted
them with great fanfare. The initial response was to celebrate the radicality
(i.e., the trauma that they represented to the traditional canon) implicit
in the mere existence of the works. The first rediscoverers grasped that
they had access to material that had long been repressed—and thus
which had said something that people were reluctant to hear. The importance of the rediscoveries, in the eyes of the initial rediscoverers, was
entirely political and consisted in bringing forth voices that had previously been silenced. Not only did these voices represent new perspec-

tives—new ways of looking at and experiencing the world—but they also represented a radical political alternative. For these critics, it was political radicality—the break from the tradition that had forgotten them—that held the key to understanding their repression. After their rediscovery, these four works became, to a greater or lesser extent in each case, political markers with which to identify oneself, signs of difference and alternatives to the hegemonic logic of the traditional canon. Each work bore its own champions, readers who grasped and articulated its political radicality, who forced others take notice of this alternative voice.

In her "Afterword" to the 1973 Feminist Press edition of "The Yellow Wall-paper," Elaine Hedges explicitly announces the publication of the story as a "rediscovery" of a work that had been previously "overlooked." The reasons behind this overlooking, Hedges implies, have to do with the radicality of the story: it was so ahead of its time that readers lacked the conceptual tools for making sense of its feminist message—and those that did make sense of it didn't like what they found. Rather than reading the story as a feminist polemic, early readers wrongly thought of it as just a horror story or a tale of mental illness. That it triggered this type of misreading—or limited reading—testifies to its radical politics. As Hedges puts it, "The story was read essentially as a Poe-esque tale of chilling horror—and as a story of mental aberration. It is both of these. But it is more. It is a feminist document, dealing with sexual politics at a time when few writers felt free to do so, at least so candidly."[56] According to this initial rediscoverer, "The Yellow Wall-paper" represented such a traumatic break from its historical situation that readers were not even able to see it for what is actually was. What they did see horrified them, precisely because of the radical feminist politics of the story. Among other things, it mounted a feminist attack "on the ideal of a submissive wife."[57] This represented a message that early readers were loath—and often unable—to hear. Hedges clearly identifies the trauma of the story in strictly feminist—that is, political—terms, which is precisely the way that enthusiasts of *The Awakening* would characterize the trauma of that novel.

The first rediscoverer of *The Awakening*, Kenneth Eble, appropriately titles his landmark essay "A Forgotten Novel." The reason for the forgetting, according to Eble, was quite clear: "The author's innocent disregard for contemporary moral delicacies ordained that it should be quickly forgotten."[58] Chopin's novel challenged traditional ideas about marriage and about sex, depicting (sympathetically) a woman who could not find satisfaction in marriage and had to look elsewhere. Edna Pontellier represented a political alternative, a radical choice of emancipation that readers of the time could not accept. As Eble asserts, "There is little doubt of the squeamishness of American literary taste in 1900," and it is precisely this squeamishness that doomed the novel to obscurity."[59] Chopin's political message—marriage is a constraint on woman, not a source of satisfaction for her—was more than such readers could stomach. The trauma of the novel, for them, was a wholly political one, stemming from their failure to countenance the possibility of female emancipation. The first rediscoverers of Charles Chesnutt and *The Marrow of Tradition* noticed something very similar, although it involved a critique of white racism, rather than sexism.

In 1974, J. Noel Heermance made one of the first significant contributions to scholarship on Charles Chesnutt with *Charles W. Chesnutt: America's First Great Black Novelist.* According to Heermance, *The Marrow of Tradition* was Chesnutt's "strongest and most savagely honest novel dealing with the racial situation in America."[60] It wasn't aesthetic deficiencies in the novel but precisely its political honesty and the searing quality of its critique of American society that led to its repression (and ultimately to the end of Chesnutt's career as a writer). It impugned white American society, and as Heermance puts it, "this is why it struck his white readers so forcefully and seared their collective guilt so fiercely that they were afraid to acknowledge any truth in the novel at all. This is why they frenetically attacked it in any and every way they could. It was that good."[61] Here, the threat that *Marrow* posed is an entirely political one: its critique of white society gave it the status of a trauma that necessitated an act of repression. It represented an alternative political vision too distasteful, unpalatable for the white majority.

The rediscovery of Zora Neale Hurston and *Their Eyes Were Watching God* wasn't put in such unequivocal terms. Nonetheless, for Alice Walker, perhaps the most well-known and influential of the novel's rediscoverers, the importance of its reemergence was clearly political as well. Walker proclaims (in a statement that one now sees printed on the back cover of editions of the novel) that "*There is no book more important to me than this one*," because *Their Eyes Were Watching God* represents a genuine alternative voice, one closer to Walker's experience of herself than any other in American literature.[62] The novel allows Walker "to enjoy [her]self while identifying with the black heroine, Janie Crawford, as she acted out many roles in a variety of settings, and functioned (with spectacular results!) in romantic and sensual love."[63] What distinguishes Hurston's novel—and what resulted in its repression—is its exuberance and self-confidence, its refusal to portray black characters as defeated (as, for instance, Wright's Bigger Thomas). As Walker puts it, "the quality I

feel is most characteristic of Zora's work [is] racial health; a sense of
black people as complete, complex, *undiminished* human beings, a sense
that is lacking in so much black writing and literature."[64] Whereas the
traumatic importance of *The Marrow of Tradition*, according to
Heermance, consisted in its attack on white society, Hurston's novel was
traumatic not for what is said about whites (who hardly figure in the
novel at all), but for the way it portrayed black characters, in a way that
confounded not only the white literary tradition, but the black literary
tradition as well. In this sense, perhaps *Their Eyes Were Watching God*
was the most radical of all the four works, because it represented a
departure from a tradition that was in itself a departure from a tradition.

However we might decide to rank the radicality of these four works
according to their initial rediscoverers, subsequent criticism has, in each
case, taken great pains to demonstrate the illusoriness of this radicality.
That is, critical correctives of these initial enthusiastic celebrations of
subversion have shown that these works did not represent the radical
traumatic break that their enthusiasts supposed. Where the initial enthusiasts saw radicality and subversion, these later critics—representatives of
the second moment of discovery—saw something very traditional. What
takes place in this moment is a revision of the revisions, a calling into
question of "facile" claims for subversion. This revisionist process tran-
spired in a similar way for each of the works, with the critical estimation
of each work undergoing the same type of trajectory—more drastic in
some cases and less so in others. In each case, however, the critical
method employed in this process varied: historicists complicated the
celebration of "The Yellow Wall-paper"; feminists dampened enthusiasm
over *The Awakening;* ethicists demanded a rethinking of *The Marrow of
Tradition;* and quasi-deconstructionists appropriated *Their Eyes Were
Watching God.*

According to this second moment of criticism, these four works are
not heterogeneous to the traditional canon, but securely belong there,
because they do *not* represent a departure from the other works that
constitute it. They can, in other words, easily be assimilated to the story
that the traditional canon tells. They are guilty of the same crimes,
capable of the same heights, and replete with the same ambiguities as
other canonical works. Rather than having the force of something traumatic or nonsensical, these works now make sense and fit comfortably
within an existing symbolic network.[65] For some of these critics of the
second moment, the very idea that these works ever disturbed readers
becomes questionable and even improbable, simply because, to them,
the works fit so well within—and even endorse—existing relations of

power within society. Far from being the ambassadors of political subversion, these works become, in the minds of some, the loci of hegemony.

Because the time for comprehending involves calling into question
earlier claims about the subversive nature of these rediscovered works,
the paradigmatic method of this second moment is New Historicism,
despite the fact that it was the prevailing critical method only in the case
of "The Yellow Wall-paper." The fundamental gesture of New Historicism is precisely this effort to rethink the idea of subversion, to call into
question its very possibility. Subversion implies a breakdown in the functioning of ideology, a chink in its armor. For New Historicism, ideology
has no such point of breakdown: it can't be subverted simply because it
produces the thing that is supposed to be subverting it.[66] The questions
that Catherine Gallagher names as central to the New Historicist project
embody to this attitude: "Was it possible, we asked, that certain forms
of subjectivity that felt oppositional were really a means by which power
relations were maintained? [. . .] Was it theoretically possible even to
differentiate the individual subject from a system of power relationships?"[67]
As Gallagher's (largely rhetorical) questions imply, New Historicism casts
suspicion on ideas of subversion, showing the way in which what seems
subversive actually supports—or even furthers—ideology. With this gesture, New Historicism exemplifies the logic at work in the time for
comprehending.

Though the time for comprehending has functioned differently in
each case (emanating from a different critical perspective), the effect has
been the same: the dulling of the traumatic edge of the work in question.
This dulling process has occurred concurrently with the widespread proliferation of the four works, and it is, in large part, the result of that
proliferation. As they become widely diffused in the culture, it becomes
increasingly difficult to cling to the idea that there is something *inherently* traumatic about the works themselves. They come to seem, in a
word, too normal to be traumatic today, and after enough proliferation,
they even seem too normal to have ever been traumatic. The result is
that critics begin to forget that these works were once forgotten and to
treat them just like any other canonical work, and in this way their
traumatic power—what the first critical moment insisted on and fought
to bring forth from the works—becomes almost completely obscured.
We can see this clearly at work in the case of "The Yellow Wall-paper."

Julie Bates Dock has spent considerable effort in debunking claims
that "The Yellow Wall-paper" was too radical for readers when it appeared. Readers did not, in this account, misread the story as a tale of
horror, but readily identified its feminist message. According to Dock,

"contemporary reviews demonstrate that the first readers did recognize its indictments of marriage and of the treatment of women, even if they did not label them with modern terms like 'sexual politics.'"[68] Feminists have posited that the story's feminist message and its overall politics were too traumatic for a nineteenth-century audience, but such a positing "casts nineteenth-century readers as purblind fools insensitive to feminist issues."[69] By providing the proper historical context, Dock is able to show that the story did make sense to its early readers, that it did not have the status of a trauma—or, at least, that it wasn't traumatic in the way that the first rediscoverers thought. She shows, in fact, that Hedges errs in her claim that "no one seems to have made the connection between the insanity and the sex, or sexual role, of the victim, no one explored the story's implications for male-female relationships in the nineteenth century."[70] If readers did actually recognize such implications, then the story was not the break from tradition that its initial rediscoverers (such as Hedges) thought that it was. Its feminism was, instead, assimilable to that tradition, as was, it turns out, the feminism of *The Awakening*.

For Kenneth Eble, Edna Pontellier represented a political alternative unpalatable to the readers of 1899, and because it presented this dangerous alternative, *The Awakening* provoked an act of repression. Edna—and the novel as a whole—broke from what was acceptable, and because of this rupture, the novel sticks out from its historical milieu. Katherine Kearns and many others of the second critical moment have taken issue with this characterization of Edna and the novel's relationship to its time. Where Eble sees a feminist sexual liberation that challenges the strictures of patriarchal society, Kearns sees instead the stale repetition of a very long, very masculine tradition. As she makes clear,

> Thinking that [Edna] crafts an autonomous self—a "solitary soul"—she vivifies instead the mummified man, a hollow Schopenhauer, an echoing Nietzsche. She awakens all the sonorous spokesmen of a long tradition of epistemological antifeminism in her repudiation of what has been defined as "maternal thinking," with its implications of inclusiveness and preservation, for a system that functions primarily by its exclusivity.[71]

Rather than departing from tradition, Edna's "radical" break actually represents an immersion into a long-established and hegemonic way of thinking. This immersion makes her indifferent—if not hostile—toward other women, who should rightfully be allies in her struggle against patriarchal oppression. According to Kearns, "Rejecting sisterhood, Edna wants what 'ordinary' women explicitly do not offer, 'the taste of life's delirium.'"[72] She rejects sisterhood precisely because she has bought into a strictly masculine ideal, entered into a masculine model of subjectivity and liberation. Her investment in this ideal, in Kearns's accounting, costs Edna both her self and possible connections with others: "Edna systematically nullifies herself as she nullifies others in her search for the masculinely defined grail."[73] Edna's story is thus not the story of feminist emancipation, but of masculinist conscription. Far from traumatizing an oppressive tradition—as Eble's account would have it—*The Awakening* is an endorsement of that tradition, an acceptance of its goal of autonomy, its disdain for other people, and, perhaps most important, its antipathy toward women. *The Awakening,* in other words, if it is emancipatory, fits into a very traditional narrative of emancipation.

The second moment of criticism on *The Marrow of Tradition* likewise contested earlier claims about its traumatic break from tradition. By contrasting Chesnutt's novel about the race massacre in Wilmington, North Carolina, with another fictionalized account (David Bryant Fulton's *Hanover*), William Gleason casts doubt on the radicality of the former. He makes clear, contra Heermance, that Chesnutt's novel was not the most radical or brutally honest one of its time tackling racism. In fact, it wasn't even the most radical novel about the Wilmington race massacre. In showing that Chesnutt's was not the most radical voice of his time on political questions, Gleason takes Heermance and earlier critics to task for apotheosizing this voice. He concludes his essay on Chesnutt and Fulton with precisely this point: "We must release Chesnutt of the burden of being the voice of both accommodation and militancy at the turn of the century. For other voices sang more fiercely, if less loud."[74] In other words, Chesnutt's novel, though it may have been a bit disturbing to some white readers, lacked the militancy or political edge that might justify us seeing it as traumatic. According to Gleason, "Chesnutt gives only equivocal endorsement" to radical politics in the novel.[75] As a writer and as a political figure, he consistently "was careful to steer a middle course."[76] This middle course, Gleason implies, was not the kind of tack that would trigger repression; this becomes especially clear when we contrast Chesnutt's novel with Fulton's, a novel which goes much further in the direction of radical politics. On the basis of this instructive contrast, it becomes apparent that if Chesnutt's novel has any traumatic importance, it cannot lie solely in the radical political position that the novel takes up. Gleason finds Chesnutt's failure to be radical further epitomized by his treatment of women in *The Marrow of Tradition*. No female characters—more importantly, no black female characters—manage to break out of stereotypical depictions. As Gleason puts it, "Chesnutt fails to shape consistently strong female images of the 'New Negro.' "[77] And Janet Miller, a potential candidate for such a role, "when she does appear in the book [. . .] is primarily seen and not heard."[78] In all aspects then—and despite its merits—Chesnutt's novel fails to rupture the tradition in which it exists. It exists within its tradition peacefully—and thus cannot be the site of an act of repression.

The second moment of criticism on Zora Neale Hurston, like the first moment, was exceptional in relation to the other three works under consideration here. Rather than criticizing *Their Eyes* for not being the radical work that earlier critics thought it to be, second-moment critics embraced the novel for its playful break from tradition. This embrace, however, places *Their Eyes* within a tradition, just as the criticisms of the three other works do, though this is a tradition of texts that break from tradition. Alice Walker saw in Hurston's work an alternative voice to even the African-American literary tradition (embodied by figures such as Richard Wright), but, for someone like Henry Louis Gates, this voice becomes a vital part of that tradition, a lynchpin in its identity, simply because the tradition itself is embodied by the idea of a break, or what Gates calls "Signifyin(g)." Though Gates does not set out to undermine Walker's proclamations about the radicality of *Their Eyes,* this is nonetheless the effect of his attempt to locate it within the tradition of Signifyin(g). Through the process of Signifyin(g), one voice both incorporates the other voices of a tradition and, at the same time, departs from those voices. Hurston's importance, for Gates, lies in her ability to represent this aspect of voice (through, for instance, her use of free indirect discourse). Hence, the novel's centrality to the tradition lies precisely where Walker saw its radicality—in its treatment of voice. Through the way in which it establishes Janie's voice, according to Gates, "We might think of *Their Eyes* as a speakerly text."[79] Seeing the novel as a speakerly text—that is, a text that makes oral storytelling and Signifyin(g) its explicit focus— allows Gates to link it to the African-American literary tradition as a whole. In fact, in the final sentence of his chapter on Hurston (as a segue into his chapter on Ishmael Reed), Gates makes this link very explicit: "If Hurston's novel is a Signifyin(g) structure because it seems so concerned to represent Signifyin(g) rituals for their own sake, then Reed's text is a Signifyin(g) structure because he Signifies upon the tradition's convention of representation."[80] Rather than sticking out—traumatically—from the tradition, *Their Eyes* now becomes part of a tradition that sticks out, and thus it loses its own traumatic edge.

In each of these cases, the same gesture is being repeated, albeit in quite different forms: critics are contextualizing the "trauma" that the earlier rediscoverers witnessed, inserting it into a narrative structure. Through the gesture of narrativizing trauma, placing it within a context, the critics of the second moment effectively cover over the trauma. They narrativize it out of existence, but at the same time, they help us to locate the trauma in a way that the first critical moment could not. In the first moment, the instant of the glance, the rediscovered works had a Real status, and it was impossible to locate what was traumatic about them. Hence, first-moment critics simply assumed that the works as a whole represented radical political alternatives that were threatening to contemporary power relations. It was, for them, this threat that led to the repression. Second-moment critics have shown, in each instance, that this was not the case, that politically these works were largely acceptable, that we can locate them within a symbolic chain. We can *comprehend* them. Though this kind of symbolization threatens to wholly obscure the trauma of the works, it has the benefit of also letting us see that trauma in a new light—as the point at which the symbolic chain fails. We can see, in other words, how the works *do not* fit into the narratives into which second-moment critics have written them, and in this way, we can once again see their traumatic importance. This time, however, we can see the trauma as symbolically located, situated as the point of the symbol's failure, rather than as a general and blinding irruption of the Real. It is precisely the task of psychoanalytic interpretation to isolate trauma in this manner, to find the point of traumatic non-sense in the midst of a symbolic chain. As Lacan puts it in *Seminar XI,* "the effect of interpretation is to isolate in the subject a kernel, a *kern,* to use Freud's own term, of *non-sense.*"[81] In "The Yellow Wall-paper," *The Awakening, The Marrow of Tradition,* and *Their Eyes Were Watching God,* this kernel, as we will see, is the inexplicable feminine "No!"—a challenge to existing symbolic authority, which, unlike most rebellions, does not root itself in a symbolically supported identity. This "No!" is a radical act insofar as it exposes the impotence of symbolic authority while at the same time undercutting the security that the symbolic order offers. Hence, the feminine "No!" is traumatic not only because it exposes the groundlessness of symbolic authority, but also because it rejects all symbolic support, even for itself. We can see this manifested in the narrator's "No!" to John in "The Yellow Wall-paper," in Edna's "No!" to her husband and to New Orleans society in *The Awakening,* in Janet Miller's "No!" to her white father's name in *The Marrow of Tradition,* and in Janie's "No!" to Tea Cake in *Their Eyes Were Watching God.* The refusal implicit in each of these acts indicates a rejection of symbolic support—a traumatic encounter with the point at which meaning fails.[82]

The danger is, however, that the narrativization of the trauma—the project of the second critical moment—will succeed and leave no more trace of its success. If this occurs, then the indications of trauma disappear and these works lose their special status. In fitting them into their critical narratives, the second-moment critics thereby prepare these works for the practice of normal criticism, by transforming them into wholly canonical works. Criticism will come to treat them exactly as it treats other canonical works, and we will soon forget that these works were ever *not* a part of the canon, that they were ever excluded or repressed. When this occurs, the opening of the canonical unconscious that they represent will definitively close, because there is only a limited window of opportunity during which a trauma remains accessible. What will ensue is the practice of normal criticism, following from the complete integration of the works into the canon. As long as critics continue to feel as though they must proclaim that the works *weren't* disruptive or traumatic, however, the window remains open, precisely because such activity indicates that they have not yet become wholly integrated: critics do not make these kind of claims (or have these kind of debates) about works well-established in the canon. While the window remains open, we can intervene with the third moment of rediscovery (the moment for concluding), but when it closes, such an intervention comes to seem unnecessary. At this point, the works would be fully integrated into the canon, completely identified with the idea of canonicity, and situated beyond the moments of rediscovery. Not only would the trauma of these works disappear, but we would have no indication that they were ever traumatic. We would, in other words, move beyond the possible third moment of rediscovery and no longer grasp that, though these works aren't traumatic now, there was a time when they were. This is why Lacan says that psychoanalysis involves making the right interpretation at the right moment. In the wake of the time for comprehending, we have reached this moment.

2

Dispossessing the Self

"The Yellow Wall-paper" and the Renunciation of Property

Fredric Jameson begins *The Political Unconscious* with the mantra, "Always historicize!," calling this an "absolute" and "even 'transhistorical' imperative" of radical thought.[1] Historicizing, in Jameson's vision, is attractive because it gives us access to trauma; it facilitates a traumatic encounter with the contingency of the present, thereby freeing us from the present's awful weight. It does this by revealing that the present doesn't owe its hegemony to transcendental necessity but to concrete historical determinants, determinants that might have been—and might sometime be—different. In short, historicizing offsets the power of the status quo. Insofar as it does this, who among the progressively minded could be against it? In the years since the publication of *The Political Unconscious* in 1981, however, another kind of historicizing has emerged: a vision of the social order without discontinuity, a regime of power without points of failure. Whereas Jameson's historicizing helped to free us from the power of the status quo and opened us to the possibility of trauma, the "new" version condemns us to the prison-house of historical continuity and closes us off to trauma. For it, there is no breaking out of the trap that history lays for us; its history is history without fissure. And a history without fissure is a history without the possibility of trauma.

Recently, criticism of "The Yellow Wall-paper" has taken up the imperative of this kind of historicizing, a historicizing that makes clear that where early feminist critics once saw a traumatic disruption of the

31

social order, we should now see the power of the social order itself.[2] A criticism that cannot grasp the possibility of the social order's failure cannot, clearly, see the feminine "No!"—itself a traumatic suspension of that order. Today, in the epoch of this historicism, the trauma of "The Yellow Wall-paper" has receded. Perhaps it is Walter Benn Michaels who inaugurated this approach to Charlotte Perkins Gilman's story, when he stated, "if 'The Yellow Wall-paper' is for me an exemplary text, it is not because it criticizes or endorses the culture of consumption but precisely because, in a rigorous, not to say obsessive, way, it *exemplifies* that culture."[3] Michaels, however, was only the beginning.

Julie Bates Dock provides a more recent instance of this historicizing, when she rejects the idea that "The Yellow Wall-paper" had an "oppositional" status within the culture. Dock asks rhetorically, "Why do critics need oppositional myth-frames in literary history to legitimize the study of a remarkable piece of writing? What is gained by identifying 'The Yellow Wall-paper' as a hitherto victimized piece of literature?"[4] Though Dock rightly points out that critics have exaggerated the degree of the story's unpopularity, she ends up downplaying the story's radicality (and the fact that it was largely ignored by publishers, critics, and readers by fifty years). Here, opposition, a moment of trauma for the social order, is consigned to the category of mythology—what Dock calls "oppositional myth-frames."[5] In this vision of the social order, gaps in that order are not really gaps, but simply another aspect of social relations of power. This vision can explain everything, everything except the emergence of new subjects within the social or the emergence of the social itself, what Joan Copjec in *Read My Desire* calls society's "generative principle, which cannot appear among these relations."[6] Just as the vision of a closed social order does not permit anything to leave this order, neither does it permit anything to enter. Without the idea (and the possibility) of a moment in which the incompleteness of the social structure becomes evident, we can explain neither how society itself begins nor how it integrates new subjects.[7]

This failure, however, should not lead us to reject out of hand recent historicist readings of "The Yellow Wall-paper" and to return nostalgically to the early feminist readings that celebrated the story as, in the words of Sandra Gilbert and Susan Gubar, "*the story that all literary women* would tell if they could speak their 'speechless woe.'"[8] The historicist readings have provided three key insights, revealing the limitations of interpretations such as that of Gilbert and Gubar. First, Dock has shown us that early readers of the story did not "misread" the feminist theme of the story. As she points out, contrary to the claims of many feminist critics of the story, "evidence indicates that [reviewers] saw Gilman's feminist message" and understood it.[9] What Dock's research tells us is that it is not simply the feminism of "The Yellow Wallpaper" that troubled readers and kept the story in obscurity for decades, but something else. Thus, Dock tells us to look beyond just the confrontation with feminism itself for the traumatic effect of this story. Second, Dock, Susan Lanser, and others have shown how feminist critics of the story have been influenced by biography—both that of Gilman and themselves—in interpreting the story. This biographical influence has produced readings that see the story as a battle of (male and female) discourses, enabling critics to extract from the story a model for feminist writing and reading.[10] Third, historicist readings have also revealed the connection between private property and the narrator's subjectivity in the story. According to Michaels, "The story of 'The Yellow Wall-paper' is a story of the origin of property and, by the same token, of the origin of the self."[11] It is the great achievement of Michaels to have discovered this link between property and self, but his great failure as well, because he insists on reducing self to property. What "The Yellow Wall-paper" makes clear—and this is what historicism misses—is that finding one's self is not a process of acquisition, but one of loss. The narrator finds her self, in other words, only as it loses its status as property. The self that she discovers, because it is not property, cannot be reduced to discourse, even a feminist discourse. Rather than being a battle between two kinds of discourse or a battle to *own* one's self, "The Yellow Wall-paper" is a story about the emergence of a subject beyond discourse and property, at the point at which both discourse and property fail, and it is this aspect of the story that has made it troubling to its readers.

The importance of property is present from the first line of the story: "It is very seldom that mere ordinary people like John and myself secure ancestral halls for the summer."[12] The narrator goes on to describe this ancestral hall as "a colonial mansion, a hereditary estate," which her and John have leased "cheaply" (29). This focus on property in the opening of the story not only establishes its centrality in the struggle for identity that ensues, but also suggests a particular relation to property in which John and the narrator exist. Because they are "mere ordinary people," they don't own the property, but are just tenants. And they occupy the property only because the natural order of things has been upset. Something supernatural has occurred—the narrator suspects it is a "haunted house" (29)—and the couple is able to live there only because its "natural" owners have abandoned the place. Thus, Gilman begins the story by stressing that the couple is in an unusual and alienated situation in their role as occupants of the property. They are not the "natural" residents; they have not inherited the property. In fact, the narrator writes that "There was some legal trouble, I believe, something about heirs and coheirs" (30). Their relationship to property is not at all proper; a gap exists between them and it. Whereas an aristocratic couple would have a "natural" relationship to the property—there would be no gap between them and it, and in a sense, the property would be a part of them—John and the narrator have an alienated, or bourgeois, relationship to it.[13] (All of the narrator's terms for referring to the property have aristocratic connotations—"ancestral hall," "colonial mansion," "hereditary estate"— suggesting further her and John's alienated relationship to it.)

Just as the couple's relationship to their house is alienated, the narrator's relationship to her self is haunted by a noncoincidence: she does not properly possess her self because it is alienated in—or, more precisely, beneath—the yellow wall-paper. In other words, at the beginning of the story the yellow wall-paper possesses the narrator's self; her self is reified in property (in the yellow wall-paper), which means that it has the status of a thing. This state of reification, which affects the identity of both characters, has its roots in the logic of capitalism and the predominance of private property. Reification creates an alienated identity, an identity that is out of joint. As Marx famously says in *Capital*, in the process of reification, "a definite social relation between men [. . .] assumes [. . .] the fantastic form of a relation between things."[14] Reification also affects the self's relationship to itself as well: one's identity acquires the character of a thing that is to be possessed. But the narrator, as the story opens, doesn't possess her self properly (just as the couple doesn't properly possess the house it occupies). This is the source of her "problem," because reification, if it is to be successful ideologically, must function unobtrusively, unbeknownst to its subjects (or, in short, it must convince people that they *really* are people, not just things). The narrator's "illness"—what necessitated this "rest cure" in the first place—is thus a sign that with her the operations of ideology aren't functioning smoothly.[15] The story establishes two alternatives for the narrator: she may, following the advice and example of John, attempt to possess her self properly, or she may, following her desire, attempt to break from this property-logic.

John preaches proper self-possession: overcome reification simply by making its processes once again inconspicuous. He is the perfect capitalist subject, because he tries to live the coincidence between property and identity, always preaching (and trying to exhibit) proper ownership of the self. The status of this ownership, however, is much more tenuous than John lets on. His sense of proper self-ownership—as does everyone's—depends upon repressing the impossibility of complete owner-ship, that there is always a part of the self that escapes one's control. John is even, on one level, aware of this, which is why he insists that the narrator abandon her desire and model herself on him. The narrator's efforts threaten to destabilize John's own self-ownership, thus making evident its problematic status, even in someone as seemingly self-assured as John. Because he recognizes the danger, John must insist unrelent-ingly on proper self-possession. In this sense, John's occupation is inte-gral to the role he plays in the story: as a doctor, he works to constitute his subject—the narrator, in this case—as an object of the rationalizing gaze, within a discourse of rationality. We can see Foucault's clinician in John. John's treatment of the narrator exemplifies the way in which, as Foucault says in *The Birth of the Clinic,* "clinical experience" attempts to effect an "opening up of the concrete individual [. . .] to the language of rationality, that major event in the relationship of man to himself and of language to things."[16] John's prescription for the narrator is for her to become like him: exhibit self-control, become the rational bourgeois subject, develop a strong and healthy ego. The narrator records this: "He says no one but myself can help me out of it, that I must use my will and self-control and not let any silly fancies run away with me" (35). The narrator's only problem, in John's eyes, is that she refuses to possess her self properly.

In advocating proper self-possession, John preaches the fundamental tenets of American ego psychology: a strong, autonomous ego and ad-aptation to the social order. Buying into this psychology is, as John makes clear, a good investment. The payoff is clear: one obtains a valu-able self about which one can feel upbeat. It requires only a simple choice, the choice of submission to the law—that is, adaptation—over one's desire. Because it demands submission to the law, the acquisition of a valuable self necessitates the sacrifice of desire. Thus, in presenting this alternative to the narrator, John inadvertently reveals a truth not of ego psychology, but of psychoanalysis. As Lacan points out in "Kant with Sade," "the law and repressed desire are one and the same thing."[17] If the narrator takes up John's investment advice and chooses adaptation, she must give up her desire. This is a price, however, that the narrator isn't quite sure she's ready to pay.

Thus, we might see the battle for the narrator's psyche that ensues as a struggle between ego psychology and Lacanian psychoanalysis, be-tween the path of adaptation and the path of desire.[18] The narrator's increasing awareness of John's malevolence indicates her movement toward the path of desire. Even near the beginning of the story, the narrator sees that John—and his insistence on self-control—might be "one reason I do not get well faster" (29). As she continues toward her desire, the narrator's suspicion about the truth of his concern becomes more concrete. At the outset she feels that "he takes all care from me, and so I feel basely ungrateful not to value it more" (30). Near the end of the story, however, she is able to articulate fully her doubts about John:

> He asked me all sorts of questions, too, and pretended to be very loving and kind.
>
> As if I couldn't see through him! (40)

What the narrator sees is simply the underside of rational self-control. This control serves only to mask an absence of freedom, a complete acquiescence to the superego's law (a law that comes, of course, from the social, the big Other). The narrator reveals John's prescription for the subject—and the demand of self-control it makes on its adherents—to be both tyrannical (it despotically governs both the self and others) and impotent (it confines one to a symbol position and thus renders agency impossible).

John's ego psychology and corresponding philosophy of identity, which view self—and wife—as property, mirror the fundamental logic of capital: both are grounded on an idea of ownership which is constantly seeking to take possession of new things. After stating that she sees through John, the narrator makes a statement that should give us pause. She guesses at the source of John's behavior: "Still, I don't wonder he acts so, sleeping under this paper for three months" (40). She sees John in the same situation that she's in: the yellow wall-paper affects both of them. Here, the narrator reiterates the connection that informs the entire story—that between property and identity. Despite his rationality and self-control, John's identity, just like the narrator's, has been subjected to the processes of reification. The only difference is that in his case the guise of self-control has deceived him and allowed him to continue to believe in the autonomy of his ego. The narrator puts this difference in her own terms: "It only interests me, but I feel sure John and Jennie are secretly affected by it" (40). The narrator's "illness"—that is, her ability to feel reification as a crisis, rather than as a tolerable state of affairs— separates her from her husband and his sister Jennie; John and Jennie are content to live as things, without bothering to notice.[19] They are content with reified existence precisely because they are convinced that they are *really* human and not just things. The narrator's radicality consists not in her being less subject to reification than John, but more so. Unlike John and Jennie, she is not plagued by the illusion that she is, deep down inside, truly human. She sees herself as a thing—as a figure in the wallpaper—and is a constant threat to reveal John and Jennie as things as well.

In fact, John's treatment of the narrator reveals that all along he has—consciously or not—been aware that the narrator's desire, if followed far enough, would reveal the way in which his rationalism has, in actuality, only a tenuous hold on his identity. Thus, John refuses to allow the narrator to reflect on herself, convincing her that "the very worst thing I can do is to think about my condition, and I confess it always makes me feel bad" (30). In a sense, John's warning here is correct: if the narrator follows the path of desire, it would be the "worst thing" *for him*. John grasps that if the narrator follows the path of desire, she would take him along with her, rendering his fantasmatic self-possession completely untenable. In his discussion of Antigone and Creon in the *Ethics of Psychoanalysis*, Lacan points out that because Antigone follows her desire to the zone that one of Lacan's students christens "the zone between-two-deaths"—the zone of freedom—she automatically takes Creon there as well: "The hero bears his partner into that zone along with him. At the end of *Antigone* Creon henceforth speaks loudly and clearly of himself as someone who is dead among the living, and this is because he has literally lost all other goods as a result of the affair. As a consequence of the tragic act, the hero frees his adversary too."[20] If the narrator frees her self, she frees John, against his will, as well (and the fact that John faints when the narrator does finally free her self indicates that this is the case). John's warning to the narrator is thus an attempt to save himself from the horror of his own freedom. The narrator, however, in her acquiescence to this warning (or order), doesn't give up her desire; she simply makes an ostensible change in object. She writes, "So I will let it alone and talk about the house" (30). As it turns out, the house is, as the rest of the story illustrates, more the narrator's self than she is, and probing the mystery of the house is not an abandonment of her desire, but an intensification of it.[21] Thus, by prompting the narrator to give up thinking about herself, John actually pushes her further down the path of desire, the path that, ironically, he is trying to block.

What follows from this turn toward the house is the narrator's attempt—which occupies the rest of the story—to free her self from its reified state, to break its connection to property. The narrator's refusal to name herself indicates her desire for a subjectivity that is not her property, that is not merely a position within the symbolic order. The

narrator's reflection on the house and the wall-paper is her attempt to
complete this break, to follow the path of desire. In a discussion of the
narrator's relation to her own subjectivity, Georgia Johnston argues that
"Through the narrator, [Gilman] shows how the woman creates herself
as text. Through her body and her authorship, the woman becomes the
subject, instead of the patient."[22] If this were true, then the thesis of
Walter Benn Michaels—that "The Yellow Wall-paper" is "an endorsement of consumer capitalism"—would surely be correct. This way of
viewing subjectivity—as textual "subject position"—misses the nature of
the narrator's attempt to constitute her own subjectivity: she does not
seek a positive subjectivity, but wants to dispossess herself, to become a
subject without any positive content.[23] It is a path on which the texts of
one's subject position are systematically exposed and stripped away, in
order to reveal the way in which one's subject position—a positive marker
of identity within the symbolic order—is a prison.

The narrator's initial descriptions of her room show it also to be
prisonlike: barred windows, a bed nailed to the floor, and walls covered
with a "horrid" yellow wall-paper. The room also forces her into the role
of a child; it served as a nursery for the previous occupants of the house.
And during the narrator's stay in the room, John begins to treat her
more and more like a child: "'What is it, little girl?' he said. 'Don't go
walking about like that—you'll get cold'" (36). Both John and the room,
as ideological forces, attempt to infantilize and imprison the narrator, but
it is the wall-paper that has the greatest effect on her. Her disgust with
the wall-paper begins with her first description: "I never saw a worse
paper in my life" (31). The paper is "repellent, almost revolting" (31).
The color, the pattern, and the condition of the wall-paper all repulse the
narrator, but what most disturbs her is its human quality. She notices "a
recurrent spot where the pattern lolls like a broken neck and two bulbous
eyes stare at you upside down" (32). The wall-paper, for the narrator, is
not simply a dead letter, but something capable of expression. Further,
she claims, "I never saw so much expression in an inanimate thing before, and we all know how much expression they have!" (32). The wall-
paper is, in a word, uncanny—or, as Marx puts it, "a mysterious thing."[24]
Marx explains that, to understand this mystery,

> we must have recourse to the mist-enveloped regions of the
> religious world. In that world the productions of the human
> brain appear as independent beings endowed with life, and en-
> tering into relation both with one another and with the human
> race. So it is in the world of commodities with the products of

men's hands. This I call the Fetishism which attaches itself to the products of labour, so soon as they are produced as commodities, and which is therefore inseparable from the production of commodities.[25]

The fetishism of commodities humanizes things. When the narrator sees human life in the wall-paper—and in "inanimate things" in general—she displays her awareness of a process that John endures unknowingly. The narrator's awareness of the humanity of things corresponds to her awareness of her own status as a thing. These are the processes she sees in the wall-paper, and it is in her relationship to the wall-paper that we can find the key to the story: her struggle against reified identity.

To understand the narrator's relationship to the wall-paper, we must understand the nature of the wall-paper itself: the yellow wall-paper has all the qualities of the symbolic order. The symbolic order is characterized by its patriarchal and discursive structure. Readers of the story have noticed both of these aspects: Sandra Gilbert and Susan Gubar see in the wall-paper "the oppressive structures of the society"; Janice Haney-Peritz sees in it "man's prescriptive discourse about a woman"; and even Catherine Golden, who sees liberatory possibilities in wall-paper, sees it discursively, as a "palimpsest" through which "the narrator comes to express herself."[26] Not only is the structure of the wall-paper both patriarchal and discursive, but its color also indicates this connection to the symbolic order. The symbolic order, too, is yellow, rather than, say, green, because everything submitted to it is necessarily petrified. As Lacan points out, "the symbol manifests itself first of all as the murder of the thing."[27] Or, as Joan Copjec puts it, no "form of life [has] ever been found to survive within the dead structures of language."[28] Presence within the symbolic order is a Real absence, the presence of absence in the symbol. The "revolting" yellow of the wall-paper is likewise the yellowing of death, which is why it repulses the narrator at first: "The color is repellent, almost revolting; a smouldering unclean yellow, strangely faded by the slow-turning sunlight" (31).[29] Though it requires the present absence of both—like the symbolic order—the wall-paper brings people and things in relation with each other. The wall-paper is a layer of mediation—literally, paper (a text) on the wall (property). It mediates and makes possible the relationship between the subject and property. It is the site of reification, the site at which people and property are linked, the site at which relations between people have the character of relations between things and things have a human quality. Though reification affects everyone, everyone does not respond to it in the same way. The narrator's relationship to reification differentiates the narrator from the other characters in the story. It is a peculiarity of the narrator's psyche, at once her "illness" and her genius, that she sees the human presence in the wall-paper and other things of the room, that, unlike the "normal" characters in the story, she sees that, in a society constructed around capital, things have more humanity than human beings do.

This ability to see what Marx calls the "mystical character" of things is, according to the narrator, an ability that she has had since she was a child. When she sees the humanity of the wall-paper, she says,

> I never saw so much expression in an inanimate thing before, and we all know how much expression they have! I used to lie awake as a child and get more entertainment and terror out of blank walls and plain furniture than most children could find in a toy-store. (32)

In the midst of her description of the human qualities lurking within the wall-paper, the narrator has recourse to a childhood experience, in which inanimate things—things created by human labor— have the characteristics of human beings (she remembers, for instance, a chair that was a "strong friend" to her [32]). These past relationships to humanized things are, in fact, the only childhood memories that the narrator relates. Her only childhood memories are of her relationship to things, which had the character of a relationship between people. Even in childhood, even in her deepest memories, there was no time prior to her seeing things with human qualities—no "human" past that has been lost.[30] The narrator does not romanticize her own childhood by positing it as a time of essential selfhood, a time of unalienated unity. Though she seeks subjectivity, this narrator is no essentialist. For the narrator (as her reflection on her childhood makes clear), things, and the relations between them, provide the model for relations between people; the relationship between things does *not* represent a fall from some primordial human relationship.

The narrator attempts, through her meditation on the wall-paper, to extricate her self—the "human presence"—from it.[31] She sees something human trapped within it: "But in the places where it isn't faded and where the sun is just so—I can see a strange, provoking, formless sort of figure, that seems to skulk about behind that silly and conspicuous front design" (33). What she sees in the wall-paper is the "ghost in the machine," the leftover of humanity existing only as a specter in a reified world. The narrator can see this specter because the wall-paper—and the

symbolic order—is not whole, but incomplete, split. Certain junctures—
"places where it isn't faded and where the sun is just so"—make possible
an insight into the human form that is hidden in the wall-paper. Furthermore, the patterns of the wall-paper "destroy themselves in unheard of
contradictions" (31), contradictions that indicate that the wall-paper does
not have a smooth and even surface. The narrator sees the human presence precisely because the symbolic order is not smooth, not a closed
loop. Instead, it gives rise to doubt, to speculation about the possibility
that its hiding something. Once again, we can see the clear link between
the wall-paper and the symbolic order. Both cannot but offer us the
illusion that they are hiding something real, something truly meaningful.
As Joan Copjec points out, *"Since signifiers are not transparent, they
cannot demonstrate that they are not hiding something behind what they
say—they cannot prove that they do not lie.* Language can only present
itself to the subject as a veil that cuts off from view a reality that is other
than what we are allowed to see."[32] Language, in other words, can never
say that it's not hiding anything—that it's telling the truth—because
such a statement always *seems* to be hiding another, deeper truth, even
when it isn't. It deceives insofar as it pretends to deceive, which is
precisely what the wall-paper does to the narrator. The wall-paper is a
lure, which is why it attracts the narrator's desire. The wall-paper con-
vinces her that there is a substantial human presence within it, but as she
comes closer to this presence, the narrator comes to recognize that it's
not all that substantial, which gives her second thoughts. At first, however, the recognition of the human presence triggers the narrator's desire. In a moment of almost complete reversal, she says, "I'm getting
really fond of the room in spite of the wall-paper. Perhaps *because* of the
Wall-paper" (34, Gilman's emphasis). She changes her attitude toward
the wall-paper because she begins to see in it the object of her desire.[33]

After days of attention to the wall-paper, the figure(s) contained
within the pattern becomes clearer: "Behind that outside pattern the dim
shapes get clearer every day" (35). This increasing clarity, however, horrifies
the narrator, prompting her once again to think about leaving the house.
She states, "And it is like a woman stooping down and creeping about
behind that pattern. I don't like it a bit. I wonder—I begin to think—
I wish John would take me away from here" (35). Clearly, the narrator
no longer desires to discover the secret of the wall-paper, but it is less
clear what occasions this dramatic change in attitude. When the form
behind the wall-paper becomes more evident, its possibility of its emergence becomes more traumatic. Following the path of desire is not an
easy road, because it weakens our sense of symbolic support.[34] As she

begins to free her self from the wall-paper, the narrator begins to feel the weight of this break. The idea that the woman behind the pattern will escape now becomes threatening: "The faint figure behind seemed to shake the pattern, just as if she wanted to get out" (36). The narrator, as Lacan would say, begins to "give ground relative to her desire," to try to escape the trauma of her desire. Though it is a prison, reified identity within the symbolic network of the Other is also a respite, providing a structural support for identity that allows one to not see the emptiness of subjectivity. As she sees the human form in the wall-paper more clearly, it becomes apparent that it is not the figure of her "true self," her "human spirit," but a senseless, traumatic form. On closer inspection, the imaginary lure—an object that would make her whole again—gives way to a figure of the Real, a terrifying form stripped of positive symbolic content. The narrator, in short, begins to see her self in its Real dimension, and she doesn't like what she sees.

The narrator sets out on the path of her desire expecting one thing—reconciliation, completion, freedom—and what she gets is something else altogether. If the narrator had known what was really lurking for her in the wall-paper, she would never have embarked upon her desire in the first place. But the wall-paper seduced her with the imaginary lure of a substantial self, of weightless freedom. Though she initially sought out a comforting identity in the wall-paper, the narrator soon discovers a traumatic one. In this sense, we can again see how close the narrator's experience is to that of psychoanalysis. With psychoanalysis—as with the wall-paper—the analysand never gets what she initially bargains for. The analyst doesn't provide what the analysand demands—relief from trauma—but rather facilitates a more thorough encounter with trauma. As Bruce Fink points out, "In therapy the therapist sidesteps the patient's demands, frustrates them, and ultimately tries to direct the patient to something he or she never asked for."[35] A subject comes to analysis, for instance, to solve marital problems, and ends up discovering that the marriage is itself the problem. We come to analysis for relief from trauma, but analysis forces us to take up the trauma as our own. The encounter with the wall-paper puts the narrator in exactly the same position. When she gets close to the traumatic emergence of her identity, the narrator has second thoughts, which is not to say she lacks courage. She gets further than most of us do. But it is not so easy for the narrator to give up on becoming subject, because she doesn't call the shots. She begs John for permission to leave the house, but he refuses—forcing the narrator back to the wall-paper.

On more than one occasion in the story, it is John's refusal to renovate or to leave the house that triggers the narrator's continually deeper attention to the wall-paper. These refusals are driven by what John considers to be economic exigencies. After the narrator's initial plea to change the wall-paper, John responds, "Really, dear, I don't care to renovate the house just for a three months' rental" (32). And later, when the narrator first begins to discern the form of the woman behind the wall-paper, John says, "our lease will be up in three weeks, and I can't see how to leave before" (36). In both cases, economic factors—and John's patriarchal authority that invokes them—force, or make possible, the narrator's following the path of her desire. In other words, it is the law itself that helps to push desire along. The power of John to compel the narrator to remain in a situation that constantly horrifies her—the power of patriarchy itself—is simultaneously the impetus for her attempt to free her self from the wall-paper. Because of her situation in this socius, the narrator has fewer opportunities to flee her desire. The horror of the rest-cure—the ostensible theme of the story, according to Gilman herself—is also the source of its potential as an engine for desire: it bars the path to the banalities of what Heidegger calls "everyday-ness," which often serve as pretexts for flights away from one's desire. The horror of the rest-cure ironically creates the possibility of the narrator's break from reified identity.[36] John's refusals of the narrator's requests for relief, the manifestations of both patriarchy and the culture of capital, make possible the very thing they are attempting to prevent—the emergence of the narrator's desire.

The fact that John's obstinacy and frugality sustains the narrator on the path of desire also reveals the contingent nature of this project. Had John been a bit more sensitive and agreed to leave the house, the narrator would have been denied the decisive break from him and his world that she makes at the end of the story. Her feminine "No!," her rejection of symbolic identity, is, in other words, something that is (at least in part) forced on her by her situation. This makes clear just how far the feminine "No!" is from Sartrean freedom. For Sartre, of course, we are condemned to freedom, unable to get away from it. As the story makes clear, the narrator has not freely decided to continue her struggle against reified identity. Her "choice" is, strictly speaking, not free: if it was up to her, she would have already given up, but the situation forces her to continue. Nevertheless, the narrator's "No!" does effectively free her from reified identity, despite the fact that it stems ultimately from a series of contingent factors. The "No!" itself, in other words, is not hers, in the sense of being her own "free" decision.

After John refuses to permit their early departure, the narrator realizes that the pattern of the wall-paper, at night, "becomes bars" (37), and she sees the woman behind them clearly for the first time. This occasions another change in attitude; the narrator no longer wants to flee the room: "Life is very much more exciting now than it used to be" (38). She once again takes up her desire, as she describes the stultifying effects of the symbolic order on the self imprisoned within it:

> And she is all the time trying to climb through. But nobody could climb through that pattern—it strangles so; I think that is why it has so many heads.
>
> They get through, and then the pattern strangles them off and turns them upside down, and makes their eyes white! (39)

Like ideology, the wall-paper imprisons the human subject, and this imprisoning produces multiple subject positions—"I think that is why it has so many heads"—points at which the subject is forced into a particular ideological role or symbolic identity. The narrator realizes that this explains why she had alternately seen "a great many women behind, and sometimes only one" (39). When she grasps that there is a self imprisoned beneath the wall-paper and that she "gets out in the daytime" (39), the narrator decides to tear away the wall-paper and free this self entirely.

Life outside of the wall-paper, however, is not exactly human. When one is outside of the imprisoning effects of the symbolic order, one is also outside of its constitutive effects, which means that beyond the wall-paper the woman has no symbolic network of support for her identity. Thus, the woman must move about like a shadow, like the living dead—"creeping"—because when she moves beyond the wall-paper she moves beyond the world of meaning. And because the act of creeping is the move of a subject without any positive content, the person who creeps can never be fully captured by the gaze:

> I often wonder if I could see her out of all the windows at once.
>
> But, turn as fast as I can, I can only see out of one at a time.
>
> And though I always see her, she *may* be able to creep faster than I can turn! (40, Gilman's emphasis)

To creep is to abandon the wall-paper, to abandon the world of symbolic meaning, and at this point the narrator wants to wholly take up creeping, which is why she is attempting to strip the wall-paper off completely.

Once outside of the wall-paper, the subject becomes an empty subject, having severed the tie to property. The move outside the wall-paper is the final culmination of the narrator's "No!"—her refusal of the satisfactions of symbolic identity.

At the end of the story, the narrator finally succeeds in freeing her self from the wall-paper. Outside of the wall-paper, we can only imagine what the narrator looks like from the effect that she has on John: confronted with a Real presence, he faints. In the narrator's last statement, directed toward John, she makes clear where she has gone. She tells him, "I've got out at last [. . .] in spite of you and Jane. And I've pulled off most of the paper, so you can't put me back!" (40). The narrator here dissociates herself from her own name—her designation within the symbolic network, the mark of her ideological interpellation.[37] The name and the symbolic mandate that it entails is precisely what the narrator has moved beyond, if only momentarily. Annette Kolodny has called the narrator's final move, not wholly inaccurately, a "liberation into madness."[38] The point is, however, that any break from a symbolic identity always has a "mad" dimension, in which one achieves a symbolic death. In *Enjoy Your Symptom!*, Slavoj Žižek discusses this escape, which he terms the "act": "every act worthy of this name is 'mad' in the sense of radical *unaccountability:* by means of it, I put at stake everything, including myself, my symbolic identity; the act is therefore always a 'crime,' a 'transgression,' namely of the limit of the symbolic community to which I belong."[39] The narrator's escape from ideology is an act of madness— and in this sense Kolodny is correct—because through it she abandons the symbolic network of support that had sustained her identity. However, unlike the psychotic, the narrator begins from the standpoint of symbolic identity and then goes beyond it. The psychotic rejects symbolic identity a priori; the narrator dies to it, and in this sense the term "madness" is misleading when applied to her.

The narrator commits herself to creeping, to a living death, which is something quite different from real death. In fact, the narrator rejects actual suicide as a means of escape after realizing that it would leave her within the symbolic network:

> I am getting angry enough to do something desperate. To jump out of the window would be admirable exercise, but the bars are too strong even to try.
>
> Besides I wouldn't do it. Of course not. I know well enough that a step like that is improper and might be misconstrued. (41)

This rejection of suicide does not indicate a last-second eruption of conformism on the part of the narrator, an indication of the narrator's concern for propriety (or for her self as *property*). As an "improper" gesture, actual suicide is the reverse side of propriety, and as such, it can be integrated into a proper world of signification. It can be made sense of—or, rather, "misconstrued." The narrator, however, aims beyond the world of construing and misconstruing, through a repudiation of even the constitutive dimension of ideology, that which secures meaning. Her break at the end of the story is, for this reason, nonsensical. Actual suicide remains something done for the Other—it sends a message to the Other, whether one leaves a note or not—whereas the narrator's symbolic suicide, her escape from the wall-paper, gives up the support of the Other altogether. It thus indicates that she has followed her desire to the point at which it becomes pure drive.

This is the point at which Gilman ends her story, the point at which the narrator completely breaks from her symbolic identity, where even her own name—Jane—is someone else. And because the story ends at this point, we have no way of knowing what the final result will be, or whether she will live out her life with John in a changed relationship, or whether John will move out of the picture altogether. In one sense, whatever happens next is unimportant, which is why Gilman stopped the story when she did (and all attempts to extrapolate an ending beyond the ending, and judge the story based on this, constitute refusals to embrace the radicality of Gilman's own ending).[40] The narrator has renounced the network supporting her symbolic identity, and in doing so, she has committed herself to an encounter with the trauma of an empty identity. This emptiness, however, is visible only when we are able to abandon the historicist vision of the social as a closed loop. Only when we see the failure of the social to constitute itself completely can we also see the narrator's achievement of emptiness—and in this way attempt to rediscover the trauma of this story, a trauma that once manifested itself in a fifty-year-long repression.

3

The Awakening of Desire, or, Why Edna Pontellier Isn't a Man

Whereas it was historicism that obscured the radicality and trauma of the narrator's "No!" in "The Yellow Wall-paper," it has tended to be certain kinds of feminism that have obscured a similar "No!" in *The Awakening*. Though *The Awakening* has so clearly been an important book for American feminism, the novel has also caused problems for those of us who have looked to it for insight into feminist politics. This is because its heroine, Edna Pontellier, "seems fully to have accepted," as Katherine Kearns says, "a masculinist definition of selfhood."[1] Throughout the course of the novel, Edna seems to discover herself as a subject, and this discovery seems to be in keeping with the traditional masculine ideal of self-possession. In the process of discovering this subjectivity, Edna seems to reject any notion of sisterhood that might bind her to other women; hers is not a communal subjectivity. Even her father, the Colonel, notices Edna's "want of sisterly affection and womanly consideration,"[2] and it certainly seems as if she devalues women insofar as she fails to achieve any solidarity with other women in the novel. This is the essence of the problem that *The Awakening* poses: Edna's discovery of subjectivity seems to imply a rejection of a female solidarity or community, the community on which a feminist politics might be based.

In an effort to sustain *The Awakening*'s significance in light of this problem, readers have attempted, in varying ways, to reconcile the novel with the ideal of a community of resistance. Most famously, Sandra Gilbert argues that, as the title of her 1983 essay suggests, Edna Pontellier is the "Second Coming of Aphrodite," a Christ-like figure in

47

"the alternative theology that haunts Kate Chopin's story of [a] 'solitary' heroine's mythologized life."[3] Gilbert puts quotation marks around the word "solitary" because, to her mind, Edna's solitude is only illusory, the result of the misperception of readers constrained by a realistic interpretive methodology.[4] Whereas Gilbert elides Edna's solitude, others simply condemn it as the mark of her inability to transcend a male paradigm of individual identity. Elaine Showalter argues that "Edna's solitude is one of the reasons that her emancipation does not take her very far."[5] Showalter claims that "Edna never moves from her own questioning to the larger social statement that is feminism" in part because she "has lost some of the sense of connectedness to other women that might help her plan for her future."[6] For Showalter, Edna is misguided because she fails to recognize a communal ideal, the importance of others. Michele Birnbaum takes this critique even further, arguing that Edna's ("traditionally Western") "possessive individualism, with its myth of the inalienable self, is precisely what makes it so difficult to see the investment in race upon which the white female subject capitalizes."[7] Edna gains her individual autonomy, in other words, only at the expense of the racialized other who is either rendered invisible or subjugated. The question is, however, Does Edna's rejection of community in the traditional sense necessarily mean that she embodies "possessive individualism"? Does it mean that, as Andrew Delbanco claims, the novel "is about a woman passing for a man"?[8]

Even those who support Edna seem to say so. These supporters simply look more positively on the achievement of individual identity. Marilynne Robinson states this position most explicitly: "In endowing Edna with a compulsion to discover her self by isolating it from all bonds that seem to her to attenuate identity, Kate Chopin has given her female protagonist the central role, normally reserved for Man, in a meditation on identity and culture, consciousness and art. This seems to me a higher order of feminism than repeating the story of woman as victim."[9] This view, although it sees Edna's discovery of her subjectivity in a more positive light than, say, Elaine Showalter's, understands the quest in exactly the same way; it simply judges it differently. Both views see Edna as the reflection of a fairly traditional idea of individuality. It is this view, which almost all critical judgments on Edna Pontellier—be they positive or negative—share, and it is this view that fundamentally misrecognizes her and misrecognizes her kinship with the narrator of "The Yellow Wall-paper."[10]

Edna does not want to be a man; what animates her, instead, is a sustained refusal of the satisfaction and security offered by symbolic identity. We condemn Edna—or applaud her for the wrong reasons—not because of her limitations, but because we insist on trying to symbolize her refusal of this kind of identity. Her refusal of symbolic identity is as far from buying into a "masculinist definition of selfhood" as is possible; it is, strictly speaking, a rejection of masculine subjectivity. Masculine subjectivity, while proclaiming its autonomy and independence from the Other, actually depends wholly on the Other's recognition. The autonomy of this subjectivity depends on the phallus, but the phallus does not belong to the male subject. Despite the fact that the subject "has" it, the phallus is always the mark of the Other. That is, "possessive individualism" does not entail possession so much as being possessed. Slavoj Žižek explains,

> if we are to assert our (symbolic) "phallic" authority, the price to be paid is that we have to renounce the position of agent and consent to function as the medium through which the big Other acts and speaks. Insofar as phallus *qua* signifier designates the agency of symbolic authority, its crucial feature therefore resides in the fact that it is not "mine," the organ of a living subject, but a place at which a foreign power intervenes and inscribes itself onto my body, a place at which the big Other acts through me [. . .][11]

The male subject, however, necessarily fails to recognize the way in which the symbolic order provides the determinations of his subjectivity. Edna, in contrast, becomes increasingly aware of these determinations as *The Awakening* progresses. Rather than simply believing herself independent of—or proclaiming her independence from—the symbolic order, Edna attempts to free herself by recognizing that she isn't free of it, which is precisely what masculine subjectivity covers over. Through this kind of recognition, she works to give up her investment in the symbolic support of her identity.[12]

Just as Edna's refusal of symbolic determination does not mimic masculine subjectivity, neither does it indicate a rejection of community. Edna's failure to bond with others—and to become a part of a community of resistance—is not her failure. It is instead the failure of every other character in the novel. For these characters, as for so many readers of the novel, "community" means a shared symbolic bond: every community, for them, is a symbolic community. A symbolic community constitutes itself as a community through harmonizing narrative, a narrative that provides a sense of coherence and wholeness to the community's identity. In other words, a symbolic community is only an illusory whole. This sense of wholeness, however, comes with a price: the Real of our desire. Edna finds this kind of community unacceptable precisely because it exacts such a costly toll for entry. Hence, she refuses the entrance requirement for symbolic community—flight from the Real—to which the other characters in the novel readily submit.

Edna's rejection of a symbolic community—even a symbolic community of women—does not imply a corresponding rejection of feminism. It signals, instead, that she takes up a different kind of feminism, a feminism dedicated not to acquiring symbolic recognition but to refusing it, saying "No!" to the blandishments of the big Other. In adopting this position, Edna makes evident the point at which feminism and psychoanalysis come together: both stem from a refusal to accept the costs of the symbolic order, its toll on the woman's jouissance. Through Edna, we can see an alternative to the path of symbolic recognition, an alternative pointed out by Renata Salecl. In *(Per)versions of Love and Hate*, Salecl says, "the subject endlessly tries to leave a mark on the Other, on the social symbolic structure, on history, etc. However, the subject can find a special form of happiness when he or she is not at all concerned with the Other."[13] The possibility of turning one's concern away from the big Other finds its exemplar in Edna, for whom the turn begins when she first recognizes this Other's control over her existence.

Chopin begins the novel at the moment when Edna first begins to become aware of her position within the symbolic order. The time of the novel's opening is also, as far as we can tell, the beginning of her dissatisfaction with symbolic determinations. Up until this time, she seems to have lived a life of relative satisfaction. However, from the very opening of the novel, Chopin points out how Léonce pushes Edna into a particular symbolic position: after Edna gets sunburned, Léonce looks "at his wife as one looks at a valuable piece of personal property which has suffered some damage" (I). Edna evinces a growing awareness of his view of her and its ramifications. While contemplating her marriage, "an indescribable oppression, which seemed to generate in some unfamiliar part of her consciousness, filled her whole being with a vague anguish" (III). This is the point at which Edna begins to say "No!" to symbolic determinations, insofar as it is the point at which she realizes, for the first time, the way in which she is subjected to them. Until she is able to feel the effects of the symbolic order upon her, Edna clearly cannot refuse them. Thus, Edna's first move toward this refusal is her cry on the porch, which occurs when she, for the first time, is not satisfied by "her husband's kindness and uniform devotion" (III). It is in this dissatisfaction that everything begins.

Edna's cry on the porch is the beginning of her refusal of the satisfactions of symbolic identity. There is clearly something "hysterical" about Edna's crying here, because it stems from her dissatisfaction with her assigned symbolic role. Hysteria is always a response to one's symbolic role, a refusal to accept quietly the master's definition of who one is. The fact that the master (Léonce) looks on her with kindness and devotion now fails to satisfy Edna. Because this kind of hysterical reaction calls into question the master's authority, it has a radical dimension, a dimension that Slavoj Žižek makes clear: "Hysteria is precisely resistance to interpellation; that is its whole point. Lacan puts it very nicely when he says, Why am I what you are saying that I am? This is the hysterical question to the master. You are interpellating me into this, but why am I what you are saying that I am? So the hysterical question means the failure of interpellation."[14] This cry on the porch, Edna's first show of dissatisfaction, is a sign that her interpellation into a symbolic identity hasn't gone so smoothly. She no longer feels herself to be identical to her symbolic mandate—her "wifeness."

Edna's hysterical refusal of her symbolic interpellation doesn't sit well with all of the readers of *The Awakening,* perhaps because it offers us food for thought about our own interpellation. Though he avoids the word, it is precisely this "hysterical" refusal of her symbolic mandate for which Lloyd Daigrepont condemns Edna. According to Daigrepont, "Edna's quest" has a "basic falsehood and unhealthiness,"[15] and she has "a somewhat immature and self-centered personality."[16] What Daigrepont finds so appalling about Edna is her "distaste" for marriage, for "marital friendship," the kind exemplified by the Ratignolles.[17] He sees their love as the one possibility for real "love between a man and woman" present in the novel.[18] Their love is perfect, Daigrepont says without saying, because it is a love freed from desire, one wholly content with the symbolic mandate that constitutes it. Edna upsets Daigrepont insomuch as she desires—and desire upsets the "harmony" of the social order.[19] The problem is, however, that this harmony—and the banishment of desire it requires—coincides with the most complete kind of domination. In *The Ethics of Psychoanalysis,* Lacan makes this point most emphatically:

What is Alexander's proclamation when he arrived in Persepolis or Hitler's when he arrived in Paris? The preamble isn't important:

"I have come to liberate you from this or that." The essential point is "Carry on working. Work must go on." Which, of course, means: "Let it be clear to everyone that this is on no account the moment to express the least surge of desire."

The morality of power, of the service of goods, is as follows: "As far as desires are concerned, come back later. Make them wait."[20]

Edna's desire puts a wrench in "the morality of power" and the functioning of the symbolic order. She confronts power with dissatisfaction.

However, Edna's dissatisfaction here does not result in any action, only in a sense of despair. Though Edna feels dissatisfaction with her symbolic identity and with her husband's authority, in the first nine chapters of the novel Edna cannot act on this dissatisfaction. This shows, in some sense, the limitation of hysteria as a political program: all the dissatisfaction in the world doesn't do anything to dislodge mastery unless it manages to manifest itself in an act. Even though she feels dissatisfaction with it, the hysteric remains ensconced within a certain symbolic position. Edna cannot act on her dissatisfaction because, at this point in the novel, she does not yet conceive of anything beyond the symbolic role into which she has grown. She feels dissatisfaction where she is, but she also feels as if there is nowhere else to go. This is why, with hysteria, there are questions, but there is never a decisive break. When Edna goes on her first swim of the novel, however, things start to change.

During Edna's swim, she swims so far from the shore that "the stretch of water behind her assumed the aspect of a barrier which her unaided strength would never be able to overcome" (X). Here, Edna has an "encounter with death": "A quick vision of death smote her soul, and for a second of time appalled and enfeebled her sense" (X). For a moment, a feeling of absolute dread overtakes Edna. It is this dread, however, which frees her, because it allows her to see the imposture of what she had previously thought to be mastery, the mastery within the symbolic order, the mastery of Léonce. It allows her to see, as Lacan puts it, that "there is no other master than the absolute master, death."[21] Before this feeling of dread seized her, Edna remained stuck in hysterical questioning, questioning that challenged mastery but which also depended on it. Despite the subversive quality of her questioning, the hysteric remains, as Slavoj Žižek points out, dependent on the master: "Hysteria has to be comprehended in the complexity of its strategy, as a radically ambiguous protest against the Master's interpellation which simultaneously bears witness to the fact that the hysterical subject needs a Master, cannot do without a Master; so that there is no simple and direct way out."[22] The feeling of dread, however, breaks through this hysterical ambiguity and shatters Edna's dependence on the master.

The dread following from Edna's encounter with her own death is important because it makes evident the limitations of symbolic mastery. It is an experience of the subject as absolute negativity, and as such, as something residing at the point of the symbolic order's failure. In his discussion of the dialectic of the master and slave, Hegel makes clear precisely how this feeling of dread works to free the slave:

> For this consciousness [of the slave] has been fearful, not of this or that particular thing or just at odd moments, but its whole being has been seized with dread; for it has experienced the fear of death, the absolute Lord. In that experience it has been quite unmanned, has trembled in every fibre of its being, and everything solid and stable has been shaken to its foundations. But this universal movement, the absolute melting-away of everything stable, is the simple, essential nature of self-consciousness, absolute negativity, *pure being-for-self*, which consequently is *implicit* in this consciousness.[23]

Dread opens up other possibilities for Edna insofar as it shows her the imposture of mastery. Though she quickly recovers from this feeling of dread, this encounter with her own death allows her to move beyond the hysterical position, beyond the abstract questioning and despair of the night on the porch. Edna's encounter with death makes possible a certain path, which, prior to this traumatic encounter, was not even conceivable. This encounter makes the role of wife visible to her, for the first time, as a role she has chosen—and is choosing—and it is the engine behind Edna's attempt to refuse this role, precipitating her first defiance of Léonce, which occurs the night of her swim.

When Edna married Léonce, she was "in the midst of her secret great passion" for "the face and figure of a great tragedian" (VII). This led Edna to see the tragedian in Léonce, to imagine a bond between them on account of her secret passion: "She fancied there was a sympathy of thought and taste between them, in which fancy she was mistaken" (VII). The subsequent realization that Léonce was not the tragedian—the breaking apart of Edna's fantasy—compelled Edna not to leave him, but to settle into a symbolic identity, in which she comes to realize "with some unaccountable satisfaction that no trace of passion or excessive and fictitious warmth colored her affection [for her husband], thereby threatening its dissolution" (VII). Chopin reveals this feeling, however, only in retrospect. From the very beginning of the novel, Edna begins to lose this sense of satisfaction; she begins to feel her hitherto satisfying identity as constraining, and thus begins to desire to move beyond it. Even after her great passion had subsided, Edna still derived satisfaction from the identity that Léonce provided for her, but after this satisfaction wanes, that identity only feeds Edna's depression. Edna's encounter with death liberates other possibilities for her; it makes clear to her the existence of a Real, something beyond the unsatisfying constraints and consolations of symbolic identity. This desire impels Edna beyond her identity as wife, and it also establishes the pattern for Edna throughout the novel: rejecting symbolic identities as they fail to provide satisfaction. What impels Edna along this path is the strength of her desire. The strength of Edna's desire dooms her to be perpetually unsatisfied with what others, in similar situations, find acceptable and even satisfying.[24] Hence, as she is rejecting her own symbolic investments, she is also constantly exposing those of others in the novel. With Edna, even more clearly than with the narrator of "The Yellow Wallpaper," we can see how her refusal of her own symbolic investment forces others to confront their own investment as well.

By rejecting her identity as wife, Edna exposes Léonce's dependence on that identity. Because it has this effect on him, Léonce—consciously at least—completely misunderstands Edna. He can see her only as ill or disturbed: "It sometimes entered Mr. Pontellier's mind to wonder if his wife were not growing a little unbalanced mentally. He could see plainly that she was not herself. That is, he could not see that she was becoming herself and daily casting aside that fictitious self which we assume like a garment with which to appear before the world" (XIX). Edna reveals the fundamental insecurity from which Léonce's symbolic identity as husband or figure of authority represents a flight and also the tenuousness of that authority. Chopin states that "Mr. Pontellier had been a rather courteous husband so long as he met a certain tacit submissiveness in his wife" (XIX). When Léonce must confront Edna's "No!," however, the facade of this courteousness disappears, and the cruelty of his authority, which that courteousness served only to disguise, comes to the fore.

As we have seen, Edna's first conscious defiance of Léonce occurs just after her encounter with her own death, and it is this encounter that makes her aware of her desire for Robert. That night with Robert, Edna feels a sensation "pregnant with the first-felt throbbings of desire" (X). Again, it is Edna's desire, here and elsewhere, which impels her to reject

the satisfactions of the symbolic world. When he returns home and Edna
refuses to come inside and go to bed, Léonce issues a command: "I can't
permit you to stay out there all night. You must come in the house
instantly" (XI). His command triggers Edna's reflection on the nature of
their relationship, but his attitude doesn't cause Edna's defiance. Léonce's
tone of voice merely provides the occasion on which Edna can make
manifest her desire. It provides the occasion for Edna to wonder "if her
husband had ever spoken to her like that before, and if she had submitted
to his command. Of course she had; she remembered that she had. But
she could not realize why or how she should have yielded, feeling as she
did then" (XI). Léonce acts as he always has; Edna, however, is not the
same Edna. Léonce's commands "appear intolerable" for the first time,
because, for the first time, Edna no longer considers herself simply Léonce's
wife. She articulates her first defiance, because she hears Léonce from a
different place. She responds, "Don't speak to me like that again; I shall
not answer you" (XI). This defiance is the first manifestation of Edna's
rejection of her symbolic identity, but it also has pronounced effects
upon Léonce. Though he had just asked Edna to come inside, Léonce
forces himself to remain awake and stay on the porch. When Edna finally
tires and decides to go in, she asks Léonce if he is coming in, but Léonce
responds, "Just as soon as I have finished my cigar" (XI). In order to
sustain his place within the symbolic order which Edna, through her
defiance, has called into question, Léonce feels that he must demonstrate
his authority—which is the essence of his identity—in an act of defiance
that must purport to be simply his own whimsy. In other words, Léonce
here feels compelled, in order to salvage his symbolic identity, to act as
if Edna's defiance had no effect on him, but this very act, paradoxically,
reveals the extent to which it did.[25]

As Edna continues to give up the security of her symbolic identity,
the exact nature of Léonce's symbolic investment gets increasingly laid
bare. When Edna leaves home for a day, without an excuse, and misses
all the callers, Léonce experiences this as a catastrophe. He tells her,
"People don't do such things; we've got to observe *les convenances* if we
ever expect to get on and keep up with the procession. If you felt that
you had to leave home this afternoon, you should have left some suitable
explanation for your absence" (XVII). When Edna dismisses the "duty"
of receiving callers as a triviality, Léonce says, "But it's just such seeming
trifles that we've got to take seriously; such things count" (XVII). Later,
when Edna informs Léonce of her decision to move into the "pigeon
house," Léonce "begged her to consider first, foremost, and above all
else, what people would say" (XXXII). His concern is that "it might do

incalculable mischief to his business prospects" (XXXII). Edna, through her own project of stripping away the narratives that inscribe her in a particular symbolic role, ipso facto strips away the narratives that sustain her husband's role, and awakens, for him as well, the possibility of confronting his own desire. Insofar as she doesn't give ground relative to her desire, she takes Léonce, her antagonist, along with her.[26] Léonce's anger at Edna is a sign that she is having this effect. In a conversation with Dr. Mandelet, Léonce illustrates the way in which Edna disrupts the peace-of-mind that he owes to his secure position within the symbolic order: "She [Edna] won't go to the marriage [of her sister Margaret]. She says a wedding is one of the most lamentable spectacles on earth. Nice thing for a woman to say to her husband!" (XXII). Edna's statement angers Léonce because it lays bare the fundamental untruth of his symbolic identity.

When Edna moves out of "Léonce's" house and into the smaller pigeon house, she realizes the break that began with her earlier defiance. This move completes her abandonment of the "wife-ness" which had hitherto defined her identity. It continues Edna's refusal of the attractions of the symbolic order, because it involves a sacrifice of her own symbolic status: "There was with her a feeling of having descended in the social scale, with a corresponding sense of having risen in the spiritual. Every step which she took toward relieving herself from obligations added to her strength" (XXXII). This also means getting rid of the servants who serve to sustain a certain symbolic status. This role that servants play is clearly evident when a maid finds the wedding ring that Edna has just tried to destroy.[27] So long as Edna relies on servants, she herself remains invested in the symbolic order and unable to free herself of its hold over her. In moving out of her husband's house, Edna gets rid of her servants, precisely because they are the mark of her own symbolic investment. As the novel progresses, Edna also takes over the dangerous tasks that others in her set relegate to the servants. Early in the novel, Chopin describes how Madame Lebrun used "a little black girl" to do all the potentially dangerous work involved with her sewing: "Madame Lebrun was busily engaged at the sewing-machine. A little black girl sat on the floor, and with her hands worked the treadle of the machine. The Creole woman does not take any chances which may be avoided of imperiling her health" (VIII). The contrast between this and Edna's attitude toward her servants is revelatory. When Arobin comes to visit her prior to her party, he finds her perilously "mounted upon a high stepladder," because, as she tells him, "Ellen [the maid] is afraid to mount the ladder" (XXIX). In marked contrast to Madame Lebrun, Edna assumes the dangerous task herself, in order to spare the servant. This contrast makes clear the path that Edna is on: the path of her desire, giving up the symbolic mandates that have hitherto dictated her existence. In refusing these symbolic mandates, Edna is led not by intellectualism but by the strength of her desire and her ability to be faithful to this desire. Because such mandates demand an evacuation of desire, she is continually attempting to move beyond them. This is true not only of her role as Léonce's wife, but also of other symbolic mandates as well.

When Edna and Robert attend church at Our Lady of Lourdes, she feels the oppressiveness of the church: "A feeling of oppression and drowsiness overcame Edna during the service. Her head began to ache, and the lights on the altar swayed before her eyes. Another time she might have made an effort to regain her composure, but her one thought was to quit the stifling atmosphere of the church and reach the open air" (XIII). Rather than ignore the oppressiveness, as she would have in the past—or not even feel it as oppressiveness—Edna walks out of the church. This action reveals that Edna has gone beyond the symbolic narrative that the church provides: it no longer holds sway over her. In the past, however, the church has been very important for her. Earlier, She had told Adèle, "during one period of my life religion took a firm hold upon me; after I was twelve and until—until—why, I suppose until now, though I never thought much about it, just driven along by habit" (VII). Habit is precisely what desire refuses; Edna's "No!" is a break from the oppressiveness of habit. As with her defiance of Léonce, Edna's flight from the church reveals, through juxtaposition, the symbolic fictions in which others are situated. Though they do not leave along with Edna, her exit reveals something about them: "Old Monsieur Farival, flurried, curious, stood up [. . .] He whispered an anxious inquiry of the lady in black, who did not notice him or reply, but kept her eyes fastened upon the pages of her velvet prayer-book" (XIII). Farival's anxiety and confusion and the lady in black's complete absorption in her prayer-book are both the products of Edna's action. Her flight disrupts the usual narrative for Farival, thus inducing his anxiety (and the possibility—not realized—that he might escape this narrative with Edna). The effect of Edna's action on the lady in black seems less clear—if anything, she seems unaffected. However, Edna actually *causes* her devotion to the church's symbolic fiction to reveal itself. Edna's refusal of this symbolic investment drives the lady in black into her complete absorption. Edna's desire, though seemingly confined to herself, has, as is clear here and with Léonce, a collective import, because it is constantly illuminating the symbolic network which structures the identity of everyone whom Edna encounters in the novel.

This is the primary reason why, in the words of Elaine Showalter's critique, "Edna never moves from her own questioning to the larger social statement that is feminism."[28] It is not because of an inability to make connections that Edna does not come to a notion of female community; it is rather that, because she rejects the "feminine" insofar as it is posited as a symbolic identity, as "substantial" being, Edna cannot bond with those who seek to sustain it and reintroduce it as a positivity to her. In one of the most well-known passages of the novel, Chopin begins to make this clear:

> Mrs. Pontellier was not a mother-woman. The mother-women seemed to prevail that summer at Grand Isle.[. . .] They were women who idolized their children, worshiped their husbands, and esteemed it a holy privilege to efface themselves as individuals and grow wings as ministering angels.
>
> Many of them were delicious in the role [. . .] (IV)

Chopin here demonstrates that "mother-woman," though undoubtedly an oppressive role, offers the individual a certain symbolic security in exchange for its oppressiveness, a security that sustains an abandonment of desire.[29] Edna, however, refuses the security of this flight; she commits herself to the Real of her desire. Edna fails to find community because the other characters in the novel who would make up this community refuse to leave the security of symbolic identity.

Just as Edna's refusal to be a wife lays bare the symbolic fiction governing Léonce's life, her rejection of the role of mother-woman effects this same process with Adèle Ratignolle, the mother-woman par excellence. Chopin describes Adèle as "the embodiment of every womanly grace and charm" and adds, "If her husband did not adore her, he was a brute, deserving of death by slow torture.[. . .] There are no words to describe her save the old ones that have served so often to picture the bygone heroine of romance and the fair lady of our dreams" (IV). Edna is not immediately alienated from Adèle, however, simply because she is a mother-woman. Edna feels, while at Grand Isle, a bond with Adèle, what Chopin describes as an emotion "which we might as well call love" (VII). This love becomes impossible for Edna to sustain not, as Katherine Kearns suggests, because

> there is a profound irony in Edna's evaluation of Adèle. For Edna seems fully to have accepted a masculinist definition of

selfhood that brings her to be "fondly" condescending toward her "intimate" friend.

In this, Edna performs an essential act of betrayal. Her gynocentric sympathies have, we know, never been allowed to develop, brought up as she has been in a stony, motherless household, but she is gradually revealed as a woman who cannot really like or value other women.[30]

It is not Edna's inability to feel "gynocentric sympathies" that severs the growing bond with Adèle, but Adèle's refusal to abandon the security of her own symbolic position (or even to sympathize with Edna's situation). Edna, unlike Adèle, cannot accept a merely symbolic satisfaction, a satisfaction as hollow as the word that authorizes it; thus, a fundamental division exists between them, which reveals, in the end, as much about Adèle as it does about Edna. This division first makes itself manifest in, of all things, the different attitudes of Adèle and Edna toward eating bonbons.

When confronted with a "box of bonbons," Adèle reacts with caution, unsure whether or not she should eat even one. Chopin makes a point of describing this caution in detail: "That lady seemed at a loss to make a selection, but finally settled upon a stick of nougat, wondering if it were not too rich; whether it could possibly hurt her" (IV). This kind of caution—that is, following the dictates of the reality principle—represents a compromise of one's desire. Adèle retreats from her own desire here. Edna, in contrast, follows her desire in the eating of bonbons, as Robert hints at when he notices Adèle's caution: "Robert started to reassure [Adèle], asserting that he had known a lady who had subsisted on nougat during an entire—but seeing the color mount into Mrs. Pontellier's face he checked himself and changed the subject" (IV). Clearly, Edna is the lady who managed to subsist on nougat alone. This indicates her refusal of caution in the face of chocolate, and it offers an early hint about the strength of her desire relative to the other characters in the novel.

Soon after Edna begins to feel a bond with Adèle in the novel, an indication of a break occurs. In an atmosphere of growing intimacy, Adèle asks Edna what she is thinking about, and Edna replies "Nothing," but immediately reconsiders: "How stupid! But it seems to me the reply we instinctively make to such a question. Let me see [. . .] Let me see. I was really not conscious of thinking of anything; but perhaps I can retrace my thoughts" (VII). Adèle, however, quickly retracts her question, not at all eager to head down the path that Edna has opened. She tells Edna, "Oh! never mind! [. . .] I am not quite so exacting. I will let you off this time. It is really too hot to think, especially to think about thinking" (VII). This thinking "about thinking" is precisely the crux of Edna's radicality. Such thinking is desire, the desire to know. But Adèle has no desire for such thought, because she feels—and wants to remain—comfortable and secure in the realm of the big Other and its assurances of what is meaningful. Adèle says here, in so many words, "Accept, don't question." Precisely because she refuses her identity in the big Other, Edna cannot accept her own reply to Adèle, "the reply we instinctively make." She realizes that her instinct, qua instinct, is not her own, but the instinct of the Other. Adèle, on the contrary, makes herself at home in the realm of the big Other, feeling herself safe in the assurance it provides. The bond between them cannot sustain itself because Edna wholly contradicts Adèle's attempt to lose her self in the Other. This disparity between them makes Edna a threat to Adèle; Edna threatens to expose Adèle, revealing that the mother-woman is a fugitive identity.[31]

So secure is she in her identity as mother-woman, Adèle can't see the possible existence of desire, even in Edna. Being a mother-woman involves a sacrifice of desire, a sacrifice that Edna is unwilling to make. When Edna and Adèle discuss their respective attitudes toward their children, they aren't even "talking the same language" (XVI). Edna tells Adèle, "I would give up the unessential; I would give my money, I would give my life for my children; but I wouldn't give myself" (XVI). What Edna here calls her self, or the essential, is nothing other than her desire. Adèle's response indicates that desire is nonexistent in her world: "I don't know what you would call the essential, or what you mean by the unessential, [. . .] but a woman who would give her life for her children could do no more than that—your Bible tells you so. I'm sure I couldn't do more than that" (XVI). Edna recognizes immediately that not only could Adèle sacrifice more than her life—that is, her desire—for her children, but that she already has. Edna responds to Adèle with a knowing laugh, "Oh, yes you could" (XVI). Adèle fails to grasp that one might sacrifice desire for one's children precisely because she has already done so thoroughly. This sacrifice creates the divide between Adèle and Edna.

This rift is made more pronounced when Edna visits the Ratignolles in New Orleans. There Edna sees, "If ever the fusion of two human beings into one has been accomplished on this sphere it was surely in their union" (XVIII). However, Adèle's bliss, as realized in this appealing union, does not particularly appeal to Edna. She sees that, in its very

perfection and contentment, Adèle's marriage, as a symbolic bond, represents a flight from desire. Edna, in fact, feels pity for Adèle, because she
understands what is lost in the contentment of a marriage like Adèle's:

> Edna felt depressed rather than soothed after leaving them. The
> little glimpse of domestic harmony which had been offered her,
> gave her no regret, no longing. It was not a condition of life which
> fitted her, and she could see in it but an appalling and hopeless
> ennui. She was moved by a kind of commiseration for Madame
> Ratignolle,—a pity for that colorless existence which never uplifted
> its possessor beyond the region of blind contentment, in which no
> moment of anguish ever visited her soul [. . .] (XVIII)

Chopin's description here reveals that Edna sees exactly what this contentment prevents Adèle from feeling—anguish. Edna herself feels anguish, because anguish follows from desire. Through holding fast to her
desire, Edna illustrates, here as elsewhere, the way in which other characters in the novel avoid their own, through a recourse to their particular
symbolic fictions, fictions that provide them with security against the
anguish of desire.[32]

Edna also reveals the cruelty that inheres in these symbolic fictions,
behind facades of friendship, care, and concern. When Adèle comes to
visit Edna after Edna's association with Arobin has become public knowledge, Adèle's character begins to reveal itself, culminating in a final and
damning revelation on the birth of her child. In an act that reveals
dimensions of her character kept hidden to this point, Adèle refuses to
risk her reputation in order to visit her "friend" Edna. Because Arobin's
"character is so well known among the men," Adèle tells Edna, "I shan't
be able to come back and see you; it was very, very imprudent to-day"
(XXXIII). Adèle ran the risk of visiting Edna on this one day not out of
friendship but out of curiosity. Consumed with curiosity to see the little
house" into which Edna has recently moved, Adèle "had dragged herself
over, avoiding the too public thoroughfares" (XXXIII). Adèle's interest
in Edna here is not that of a friend, but of a curiosity seeker.[33] Once this
curiosity is sated, Adèle won't be back, unwilling to risk an appearance
at Edna's house. Because she refuses to risk the security of her symbolic
identity, Adèle is incapable of being a friend to Edna. Underneath her
friendship is cruelty, the unintentional cruelty of someone wholly committed to the dictates of the big Other.

The full impact of this cruelty is unleashed in Adèle's final words to
Edna. Immediately after having given birth, Adèle tells Edna, "Think of

the children, Edna. Oh think of the children! Remember them!"
(XXXVII). With this seemingly innocuous plea, Adèle delivers a devastat-
ing blow to Edna. Here is revealed completely the cruelty that makes
itself manifest in symbolic identity: not only does Adèle not want to
escape this identity herself, but she cannot permit (and this is the essence
of the symbolic investment, why it is precisely an *investment*) anyone else
to escape it either. For Adèle, Edna's "No!" constitutes a threat to the
security of the symbolic identity itself, because she denatures that identity. We see clearly now that it is not Edna's blindness or her limitations
but rather this social aspect of her refusal itself that prevents her from
realizing communal bonds with other women. Even more than with
Adèle, such a bond seems possible with Mademoiselle Reisz, but once
again, it cannot be realized because Mademoiselle Reisz, in the last instance, lacks the strength of Edna's desire—she "gives ground relative to
her desire"—and thus refuses to go where Edna does.

Mademoiselle Reisz and Edna seem, at first, to be kindred spirits.
After playing the piano for their group on Grand Isle, the former tells
Edna, "You're the only one worth playing for. Those others? Bah!" (IX).
And later, Chopin describes this bond further: Mademoiselle Reisz
"seemed to echo the thought which was ever in Edna's mind; or, better,
the feeling which constantly possessed her" (XVI). However, this bond,
though stronger than the one between Edna and Adèle Ratignolle, shares
its fate, because though Mademoiselle Reisz challenges certain symbolic
fictions (she is a woman living alone and seems to be an artist, one who,
in her own words, has "the soul that dares and defies" [XXI]), she
refuses to follow her desire wherever it might take her.[34] The difference
between the attitude of Mademoiselle Reisz and Edna toward the ocean
is significant in this light, especially because of the ocean's metaphoric
importance in *The Awakening*. Whereas Edna ventures far into the sea
even though "a certain ungovernable dread hung about her when in the
water" (X), Mademoiselle Reisz refuses to get in the water. Chopin only
offers assorted opinions about the reason: "Some among them thought
it was on account of her false hair, or the dread of getting the violets wet,
while others attributed it to the natural aversion for water sometimes
believed to accompany the artistic temperament" (XVI). Swimming far
away from the shore, for Edna, brings about an "encounter with death"
(X); it is this encounter that Reisz shies away from. Mademoiselle Reisz,
though she tells Edna that she must "possess the courageous soul [. . .]
the soul that dares and defies" in order to succeed as an artist, does not
herself possess this kind of courage. And she lacks Edna's courage, simply
because she lacks the strength of Edna's desire.

Edna is not, as many critics have surmised, a mean or a "tension between Adèle Ratignolle's code of affiliation and the politics of separation of Madame Reisz."[35] Edna is not a compromise, less integrated in society than Adèle but more so than Mademoiselle Reisz; instead, she goes beyond the constraints that bind both characters. She transcends Reisz, and exposes her symbolic investment through the contrast between the two of them. Their discussion about Edna's love for Robert is revelatory. Reisz disagrees with Edna's "choice" in Robert: "It seems to me if I were young and in love I should never deem a man of ordinary caliber worthy of my devotion" (XXVI). She asks Edna, "Why do you love him when you ought not to?" (XXVI). Reisz's inability to understand Edna's desire, her wish that it concern itself with the good (and with goods), reveals the paucity of her own. Lacan makes clear the opposition between the good and desire: "The sphere of the good erects a strong wall across the path of our desire. It is, in fact, at every moment and always, the first barrier we have to deal with."[36] Reisz tries to convince Edna to "give ground relative to her desire" for the sake of the good: desire gets in the way of the good, which is why Reisz is so wholly opposed to it. Desire gets in the way of acquiring goods and garnering symbolic status. Reisz tells Edna that she would have fallen in love with "a man with lofty aims and ability to reach them; one who stood high enough to attract the notice of his fellow-men" (XXVI). Despite her antisocial appearance and demeanor, Reisz reveals here a fundamental preoccupation with acquiring the recognition of the Other, through attaching herself to a well-positioned man. During this conversation, Edna's desire to overcome the limitations of her own symbolic position reveals most pointedly the limitations of Reisz's—and Reisz's refusal of desire. Clearly, then, it is not Reisz's refusal to integrate into society that prohibits a bond between Edna and her, but the very strength of this integration itself.[37]

Just as Edna's desire makes impossible any bond with other women in the novel, it also destroys the possibility of a union through romance or love with a male character as well. Her extramarital relationships with male characters—Arobin and Robert—do, however, tell us something about Edna. The very fact of Edna's affair with Arobin is a sign of how far Edna has come. At the beginning of the novel, she exhibits "prudery," blushing at the slightest allusion to sexuality (IV); however, later, when she first kisses Arobin, Chopin points out that Edna feels "neither shame or remorse" (XXVIII). This transformation is one of the indications of Edna's refusal of the symbolic fictions that hitherto animated her existence. Thus, it is Edna's fidelity to her desire that makes her relationship with Arobin possible; yet it is also what, at the same time, makes it impossible as well. Edna is incapable of being satisfied within the confines of a symbolically determined relation, even an adulterous one. This dissatisfaction is the source of her ability to expose the symbolic investment of Arobin (and Robert). Arobin, who has a reputation—both Adèle and Dr. Mandelet are aware of it—for seducing women, exhibits a "manner that was so genuine that it often deceived even himself" (XXV). Though she accepts his advances, Edna's interaction with Arobin constantly exposes his deceptions and flatteries. When he is about to tell her "what manner of woman" she is, Edna stops him: "Oh yes! You will tell me that I am adorable; everything that is captivating. Spare yourself the effort" (XXVII). Edna sees through Arobin's flattery. This is not simply her way of rejecting his advances—she doesn't—but a recognition of them that refuses to accept them at face value. Later, when Arobin tells her, "You know that I only live when I am near you," Edna sees that Arobin is only reenacting a role that he was played many times: "Is that one of the things you always say to women?" (XXXIV). Arobin is nothing but the symbolic role—that of seducer—which he plays, and Edna is constantly making such roles uncomfortable for those around her to inhabit.

Her refusal of symbolic fictions is also the force which, in the end, makes her relationship with Robert impossible. When Robert, with a kiss, confesses his love for Edna, his ensuing remarks demonstrate a typical vision of love. He tells Edna, "Something put into my head that you cared for me; and I lost my senses. I forgot everything but a wild dream of your some way becoming my wife" (XXXVI). Edna responds indignantly, "Your wife!" and then completely undercuts Robert's position: "You have been a very, very foolish boy, wasting your time dreaming of impossible things when you speak of Mr. Pontellier setting me free! I am no longer one of Mr. Pontellier's possessions to dispose of or not. I give myself where I choose. If he were to say, 'Here, Robert, take her and be happy; she is yours,' I should laugh at you both" (XXXVI). Even though her desire for Robert has been, to this point, part of what has driven her, she is able, with this statement, to destroy his entire conception of love. Thus, the one bond that Edna held out as a possibility for herself is made impossible through the force of Edna's own refusal of symbolic fictions. When Robert realizes that he cannot possess Edna, he flees. His "love" cannot withstand the force of Edna's attack. None of the other characters in the novel, even Robert, exhibits Edna's commitment to her refusing symbolic determinations, because each recoils from the risks that it implies. Edna, on the other hand, takes these risks because she does not give up on her desire, and this desire enables her to reveal the hidden dimensions of every symbolic identity (husband, wife, seducer, lover, mother-woman, artist, believer, etc.).

The engine driving Edna is her fidelity to her desire. However, as the novel concludes, Edna comes to a new realization about her own desire: "There was no one thing in the world that she desired. There was no human being whom she wanted near her except Robert; and she even realized that the day would come when he, too, and the thought of him would melt out of her existence, leaving her alone" (XXXIX). She realizes here not only her fundamental isolation but also that her desire will constantly remain unsatisfied, because it can never attain fulfillment in its object. This realization is consonant with a movement, in Lacan's terms, from desire to the drive. In the drive, we no longer have the hope that sustained us in our desire.[38] The object is constitutively lost in the drive, and thus the drive is a pursuit without hope. As Lacan says, "It is not that desire clings to the object of the drive—desire moves around it, in so far as it is agitated in the drive."[39] But because the drive is the pursuit of a lost cause, Edna is unable to sustain it. At the moment when desire turns into drive for Edna, when she recognizes that "there was no one thing in the world" that would give her satisfaction, Edna abandons her desire and gives up her refusal of symbolic consolations. Once Edna can no longer hope, she "gives way relative to her desire." Her project all along has been to move beyond the determinations of the Other, and yet, Edna cannot sustain it without the hope of fulfillment.

Edna's final act, her drowning, is neither—as critics would alternately have it—her victory as an individual subject nor her defeat by societal forces; it is rather the culmination of her retreat from desire into fantasy. In this final act, Chopin shows us Edna's retreat from the drive into symbolically sustained fantasy. Fantasy is the attempt to fill in the lack or desire of the Other with one's own lack, in order to eliminate or transcend desire. Through fantasy, one can get one's bearings vis-à-vis the horrible ambiguity of the Other's desire. In short, fantasy provides the illusion of transcending the symbolic order without the torment involved with desire. In the novel's final scene, Edna seems to be completely discarding and moving beyond the constraints of the symbolic order:

> Edna had found her old bathing suit still hanging, faded, upon its accustomed peg.

> She put it on, leaving her clothing in the bath-house. But when she was there beside the sea, absolutely alone, she cast the unpleasant,

pricking garments from her, and for the first time in her life she stood naked in the open air [. . .] (XXXIX)

Not only is Edna shedding the constraints of clothing here, but Chopin's phallic imagery—the "peg" and the "pricking" garments—also suggests that she is transcending the patriarchal symbolic order. Her nakedness makes Edna feel like a "new-born creature," and she seems to have achieved an originary subjectivity, moving beyond the Other. This vision of the complete transcendence of the Other fundamentally deceives because it views symbolic determinations as external limitations that can simply be taken off—like clothes—rather than as constitutive.[40] With the closing images of the novel, Chopin makes clear that though Edna seems to have finally realized her desire, she has instead engaged in the fundamental self-deception of fantasy. Fantasy offers the illusion of the possibility of desire's realization, but fantasy also, unlike desire, is an imaginary reconciliation.[41]

The final images in the novel recall Edna's youth: her father, her sister, the chained dog, the cavalry officer, and the field. In each of them, the security of the symbolic order manifests itself. Her father is a patriarchal force more stern—and secure—than Léonce. Her sister is the traditional mother-woman. The dog, chained and aged, is a figure of security and servitude. As these first three images of the novel's final paragraph indicate, Edna dreams of being home again, of losing her self, as she was wont, in the Other. The cavalry officer is perhaps the most important of these images, because he was one of a series of Edna's childhood "passions." Her behavior toward him and her other passions suggests a fantasy of self-loss: "She could not leave his presence when he was there, nor remove her eyes from his face" (VII). Léonce and Robert were also part of this series; Edna continually invested her self in each new object of her passion, from the cavalry officer, to a young gentleman, to a tragedian (for whom she mistook Léonce), to Robert. With each successive love-object, Edna loses her self in fantasy anew. These passions served Edna as a way of losing her self and trying to escape desire. This fantasy of escape thus coexisted, for Edna, all along with her desire.

The Awakening is a working out of this relation between fantasy and desire and a depiction of their constant struggle. They are engaged in this constant struggle because fantasy both gives shape to our desire and is a flight from that desire. As Slavoj Žižek puts it in *The Sublime Object of Ideology,*

> *Through fantasy we learn "how to desire."* In this intermediate position lies the paradox of fantasy: it is the frame co-ordinating

our desire, but at the same time a defence against [desire], a screen concealing the gap, the abyss of the desire of the Other. Sharpening the paradox to its utmost—to tautology—we could say that *desire itself is a defence against desire*: the desire structured through fantasy is a defence against the desire of the Other, against this "pure," trans-phasmatic desire (i.e., the "death drive" in its pure form).[42]

This double aspect of desire is most evident in the figure of the sea. In one sense, the sea offers Edna the fantasy of reconciliation with the whole—an "unlimited in which to lose herself" (X). In another sense, however, the sea makes possible "her encounter with death" (X), which appalls and enfeebles Edna. The "encounter with death" that took place during Edna's earlier swim only occurs when Edna "turned and looked toward the shore" (X), something she does not do on her final swim in the novel. This turn back toward the shore indicates that Edna is following the path of the drive. The drive doesn't remain with its object, finding satisfaction in that way, but always returns, finding satisfaction through its path alone, not its object. This is precisely how Lacan describes the drive: the drive goes around the object and then returns; it goes out into the ocean and then turns back toward the shore, in order that it can continue to repeat its pulsating movement. It is this return— the turn back to the shore—that is missing both in fantasy and in Edna's final swim. Edna remembers the turning back of her earlier swim and recalls that "the terror seized her at the fear of being unable to regain the shore. *She did not look back now, but went on and on*, thinking of the blue-grass meadow that she had traversed when a little child, believing it had no beginning and no end" (XXXIX, my emphasis). In refusing the returning movement of the drive, Edna takes flight into fantasy—an imaginary union with the infinite, a respite from her own finitude. This time, the sea, as Helen Emmitt puts it, "does not leave her alone."[43]

In the final chapter, Chopin shows that for Edna, the fantasy of losing her self in the "green meadow" and "*ocean* of waving grass" (VII, my emphasis) of her childhood, with its "hum of bees" and "musty odor of pinks" proves stronger than her desire, once her desire became hopeless, that is, once her desire became drive (XXXIX). In the last instance, Edna fails to arrive at the place occupied by the narrator of "The Yellow Wall-paper"; Edna can not take her "No!" quite that far. Her suicide, rather than indicating a rejection of the Other, suggests a fantasmatic immersion into it. And fantasy provides a solace, a comfort, that the drive does not. This is why, as Jean Wyatt rightly points out, "Edna's

connection with the sea proves more fulfilling than her relationship to
any of the men."[44] Edna exhibits more of desire than any other character
in the novel, but even this, finally, cannot equal the image of reconciliation that fantasy has to offer. In this final chapter, however, Chopin is
not rejecting the idea of holding fast to one's desire as an impossibility.
She is, instead, providing us with, at least at the end of the novel, a
negative example. Chopin does this by, in a sense, doing to Edna what
Edna has done to the other characters in the novel—that is, revealing the
way in which they abandon desire. Though it does finally fail, Edna's
project in the novel has a clear political dimension, in that it forces us
to recognize the nonexistence of the big Other, the substancelessness of
symbolic determinations we rely so heavily on. Through Edna, we can
grasp the contours of the political importance of the feminine "No!"—
the political importance of the traumatic encounter—an importance that
becomes even more pronounced in Charles Chesnutt's *The Marrow of
Tradition,* an avowedly political novel.

4

Acting without the Father

Charles Chesnutt's New Aristocrat

If both Gilman and Chopin seemed at first politically suspect, this seems to be even more the case with Charles Chesnutt. Upon his recent emergence as an important figure in not only African-American but American literature on the whole, Chesnutt has come under attack for his political accommodationism, his classism, and even his intraracial racism. The focal point of these attacks is often what William Andrews calls Chesnutt's "magnum opus": *The Marrow of Tradition*. Criticism targets this novel before others because it is Chesnutt's first decidedly political novel and also the one most openly so. It fictionalizes the Wilmington, North Carolina "race riot" of 1898, depicting two primary African-American responses to white aggression: William Miller's accommodationism and Josh Green's militant resistance. P. Jay Delmar argues that with this very depiction, "Chesnutt had painted himself into an 'either-or' corner," which "reveals the limitedness of his vision."[1] Others have been even less forgiving, because they see—and this is, according to William Gleason, the contemporary critical consensus—that William Miller is "Chesnutt's more likely spokesperson [than Josh Green]."[2] Though he sees that Chesnutt "respects both men" and regards both of their historical roles as important, William Andrews, who describes Chesnutt as a player of "accommodationist literary politics," stresses Chesnutt's identification with Miller.[3] In *The Literary Career of Charles W. Chesnutt,* Andrews tries to show that "not only is Miller's philosophy vindicated practically; it is also defended on moral grounds."[4] Gleason accuses Chesnutt of waging a "safer war" than his contemporaries, because his "narrative suggests that he sees more promise in Miller's 'Give it up boys, and wait,' than in Josh's eagerness to fight."[5] Sally Ann Ferguson takes the condemnation of Chesnutt even further, seeing in the characterization of Josh Green an implicit sign of Chesnutt's racism (which she links to his belief in amalgamation as the solution to the "race problem"): he "kills off the static, black, and violent Green."[6] These critiques (and almost every interpretation of the novel)[7] stick upon the Green/Miller opposition, what Delmar calls the novel's "moral dilemma," and attempt to mediate or account for this dilemma. What they miss—and this has crucial ramifications—is that, on one level, *there is no difference between Miller and Green* and that this is precisely the key to the traumatic dimension of the novel. It is only by transcending this opposition that we can see the kinship between *The Marrow of Tradition* and the texts of Gilman and Chopin.

In focusing on the distinction between Miller and Green, such critiques miss the fact that both of their responses to the white violence share a fundamental element (deeper than their mutual ineffectiveness): neither escapes the shadow of the symbolic Father (the white man, in Miller's case, and the literal father, in Green's). The Father, in both cases, determines the response of each character to the white violence: Miller doesn't want to anger the white man; Green wants to avenge his father (who was killed by the Captain McBane and the Klan). Both of these responses remain within the symbolic universe of the situation they are attempting to negate and transcend—the "race riot." The point here is not that Miller's accommodationism succeeds—or that Chesnutt "endorses" it—where Green's militancy fails but that both actions fail and that both actions are not really actions at all, but reactions, caught within the symbolic web of the Father. In other words, in the case of both Miller and Green, a clear symbolic cause motivates their (re)actions; they are the effect of this cause, just as they are ineffective. These two characters, however, are not the only ones in the novel who attempt to act in the face of racial violence. In fact, *Marrow* is in some sense a novel of the act, exploring the very possibilities of ethical or political action. In the unlikely character of Mr. Delamere, an ex-slaveholder, Chesnutt depicts the novel's only—with one critical exception—successful act: that of saving Sandy Campbell from the lynch mob. The aristocratic Mr. Delamere, in the contrast to the other characters that populate the novel, is able to realize *his* desire against the tide of external events. Delamere does not react to the determinations of some symbolic Father but is able to act, because he views himself as a symbolic Father. This view of himself enables Delamere to signify a break in the causal chain of history: there is no symbolic cause of his act. His act is constituted on this break in the chain of causality, and thus the act forces on him a burden of responsibility.

Delamere, as an aristocratic ideal, occupies the ethical center of *Marrow*. The irony here is obvious: because the good white characters are old aristocrats (Samuel Merkell, Olivia Carteret's father, in addition to Delamere), the novel seems to be a work of nostalgia, specifically nostalgia if not for the days of slavery, then at least for the aristocratic slaveholder. The aristocrat, the character most directly responsible for slavery, seems to be the only one capable of healing its wound.[8] Only the aristocrat can, it appears, become subject qua agent, because only the aristocrat can realize himself as the cause of the social reality. It is, in other words, the particular disposition of the aristocratic mind-set to see the social reality not as something alien and imposed on it but as the manifestation of its desire. Delamere exhibits this very disposition in his attempt to free Sandy:

> we [white America] thought to overrule God's laws, and we enslaved these people for our greed, and sought to escape the manstealer's curse by laying to our souls the flattering unction that we were making barbarous Negroes civilized and Christian men. If we did not, if instead of making them Christians we have made some of them brutes, we have only ourselves to blame, and if these prey upon society, it is our just punishment![9]

For Delamere, the racial tension in Wellington—the social reality itself—has its cause not in "Nigger domination" (as Captain McBane would have it) but in his own agency; he has caused the social reality to be what it is. This responsibility in turn allows Delamere to believe that his desire is always capable of realizing itself, even when the social reality seems at its most antagonistic—when the mob prepares to lynch Sandy. When he first hears of the threat of a lynching, Delamere tells William Miller, "There'll be no trouble after I get there, William" (200). The novel's other characters, in contrast, feel the social reality as an overarching antagonist, as that which resists their desire and short-circuits its realization. They either blindly follow the tide of history and are merely the effect of the social reality (the lynch mob), or they react in vain to history's antagonistic force (Miller and Green).[10]

Delamere sustains the connection between his desire and its realization as social reality because he is what Slavoj Žižek calls the classical Master. According to Žižek, "The authority of the classical Master is that of a certain [. . .] signifier-without-signified, auto-referential signifier which embodies the performative function of the word."[11] This Master's name alone has agency, has the power to effect a change in the social order. Hegel's theorization of the monarch in the *Phenomenology of Spirit* also details the performative power of the monarch's word:

> In the name, the individual *counts* as a pure individual, no longer only in his consciousness, but in the consciousness of everyone. By his name, then, the monarch is absolutely separated off from everyone else, exclusive and solitary; as monarch, he is a unique atom that cannot impart any of its essential nature. This name is thus the reflection-into-self, or the *actuality* which the universal power has *in its own* self; through the name the power is the monarch.[12]

The power of the master (the monarch) is present in the very name; thus, because the name always realizes itself as the social reality, there is, for the master, no disjunction between his or her desire and the social reality. In his mind, there is nothing Delamere—with his name—can't accomplish. When he first hears about Sandy's imprisonment, this attitude can be seen in full flower. He says to William Miller, "Just tell them I say Sandy is innocent, and it will be all right" (199). Later, in a speech to Carteret, Delamere again invokes this "performative function of the word" in affirming Sandy's innocence: "Time was, sir, when the word of a Delamere was held as good as his bond" (211). In this instance, however, Delamere's word is not enough to free Sandy; Carteret's reply to Delamere's request—"On your bare word, sir?" (211)—reveals that the name of the old Master (the Name of the Father) has lost its performative capability. Delamere himself realizes this when he laments, "I fear I have outlasted my epoch" (211). Confronted with this new epoch, where the inherent aristocratic authority of the past has lost its efficacy, the name "Delamere" alone is not enough to prevent the lynching. As Joyce Pettis notes, "The notion of noblesse oblige, commonly associated with the aristocrat, finds its expression in Old Mr. Delamere, but it is impotent in confrontation with changed racial attitudes."[13] Though his name has lost its performative power, Delamere is nonetheless able to prevent the lynching, to act against the tide of history. And Chesnutt clearly contrasts this ability with the inability of the novel's other characters, titling the chapter which depicts their failed efforts, "How Not to Prevent a Lynching."

It is, however, only through the renunciation of his name—sacrificing his aristocratic position as the Master Signifier—that Delamere enacts

Sandy's release from prison. Delamere sacrifices his own grandson; as he tells Carteret, "Tom is no longer a member of my family. I disown him. He has covered the family *name*—my *name*, sir—with infamy. We have no longer a family honor. I never wish to hear his *name* spoken again!" (228, emphasis added). After disowning his name, Delamere appeases the lynch mob with a lie—swearing that Sandy was with him the previous night. With this renunciation and final lie, he forsakes the authority of his name and the aristocratic disposition disappears from the novel. The loss of the name deprives Delamere of the most important aspect of his authority. In the *Philosophy of Right,* Hegel articulates, in his discussion of the monarch's authority, the importance of the name. He says that the monarch "has often no more to do than sign his name. But this name is important. It is the last word beyond which it is impossible to go."[14] Since the monarch's authority is wholly symbolic—as is Delamere's— everything is lost with the name. Even though the mob never discovers Delamere's lie, it destroys his symbolic authority because Delamere himself can no longer believe in it. Delamere had authority not merely because everyone else believed that he did, but also because he believed.[15] Without this belief, which enables him to conceive of his own responsibility for the social reality, Delamere loses his status as an authority. This is the moment of Delamere's and the aristocrat's symbolic death (and his literal death, which occurs soon afterward, is but a formality).

In an ostensibly historical novel concerned with the Wilmington "race riot," the inclusion of the near-lynching and rescue of Sandy seems to be, at best, superfluous to the narrative line. It seems to substantiate William Andrews' claim that in *Marrow* "there is no slighting of opportunities for melodrama."[16] The melodramatic air of this incident, however, belies its formal necessity. Through this scene, Chesnutt reveals precisely what could (but would not) prevent the November massacre: the aristocratic act. But Delamere's renunciation of his name, which saves Sandy, strips his word of its performative power and occasions his symbolic death. (His lie to the lynch mob reveals—to himself—that his word is no longer at one with the social reality; it reveals, in short, an unbearable gap.) And in the wake of the aristocrat, there is no longer an agent to resist the white brutality.[17] The death of the aristocrat—the one *responsible* for slavery—is the very thing that seems to make it seem impossible to resist the effects of slavery. Chesnutt includes the "melodramatic" Delamere/Sandy subplot in order to highlight this truth. Nonetheless, it is a point at which readers tend to balk. William Andrews, for instance, criticizes the aesthetic value of Sandy Campbell and Mr. Delamere:

Sandy Campbell could find a home in any of Thomas Nelson Page's fictional plantation mansions, so faithfully is he reproduced in the loyal retainer mold. His master, Mr. Delamere, the reader is informed, also survives as "an interesting type" along with other holdovers from popular southern fiction which Chesnutt appropriated to give his novel the appearance of local color accuracy.[18]

The fact that Mr. Delamere is a type is not a sign of the weakness of Chesnutt's imagination or the result of Chesnutt writing a "purpose novel," but precisely the novel's most radical point.[19]

Delamere is a type that is no longer possible, and this, more than anything else, allows the massacre to go unimpeded. With the loss of the aristocrat, the loss of the exception, the name of the Master that remained outside of the circuit of exchange, there occurs a loss of the possibility of the act. This is why, in the *Philosophy of Right*, Hegel argues for the necessity of the monarch, even within an otherwise democratic state.[20] The monarch, like Delamere, "by saying 'I will' makes its decision and so inaugurates all activity and actuality."[21] Only the monarch is capable of the originary act that is not merely a reaction, "something not deduced but purely self-originating."[22] Without the monarch constituted as an exception to the social totality, this act would be impossible and the monarch would be condemned to mere reactivity. As Hegel says, "This ultimate self-determination [of the monarch . . .] can fall within the sphere of human freedom only in so far as it has the position of a pinnacle, explicitly distinct from, and raised above, all that is particular and conditional, for only so is it actual in a way adequate to its concept."[23] The freedom of the monarch, the possibility of his or her act, depends on this position outside the symbolic universe—as its exception. But with the loss of the monarch's exceptionality, social reality becomes (for everyone) an utterly antagonistic force that imposes itself on individuals, who either mindlessly act out its will or resist without avail.[24] What Chesnutt depicts through this loss is the deterritorialization apropos of capitalism, a deterritorialization which uproots the authority of the classical Master—the performative power of his name—by revealing that this Master's authority is but an illusion, that even the Master cannot escape the circuit of exchange.[25]

Through the other characters in *Marrow,* Chesnutt reveals the exact dimensions of what is lost with the death of Delamere, the aristocratic Father. Without this Father, subjective agency can no longer be active, but becomes condemned to a cycle of reactivity. Even the "Big Three," the most tangible force behind the massacre, do not view themselves as acting, but as reacting to a threat of "nigger domination." Chesnutt describes the paranoiac mindset of the Big Three:

> It remained for Carteret and his friends to discover, with inspiration from whatever supernatural source the discriminating reader may elect, that the darker race, docile by instinct, humble by training, patiently waiting upon its as yet uncertain destiny, was an incubus, a corpse chained to the body politic, and that the negro vote was a source of danger to the state, no matter how cast or by whom directed. (80)[26]

For Carteret, General Belmont, and Captain McBane, their actions are merely the response to an external cause—the "threat" they perceive. After the death of Polly Ochiltree, for instance, Carteret feels that "the whole white womanhood of the South is in danger" and that "Wellington is in the hands of negroes and scalawags" (182, 183). The Big Three never function as agents in the novel because their actions always have this reactive character. They ironically believe they are reacting against the oppressive weight of history at the exact moments they are most doing its bidding.[27] But for them (and this is why they are fundamentally reactive characters), history is always external, always "out there." Carteret is, clearly, the individual with the most power in Wellington: he and his small contingent almost singlehandedly initiate the massacre. And yet, Carteret's self-perception is quite different than old Mr. Delamere's; he sees himself not as Master (as did Delamere) but as victim. He sees history as an antagonistic force that threatens to overrun Wellington and all the institutions he cherishes.

This contrast between Delamere and Carteret is also evident in each of their attempts to intercede in white-on-black violence. By (falsely) swearing that he was with Sandy, Delamere is finally successful in averting the lynching; Carteret, however, after the massacre that he helped to initiate becomes too bloody for his tastes, attempts in vain to quell the violence. He tells his assistant Ellis, "This must be stopped [. . .] They are burning houses and killing women and children.[. . .] We must try to stop this thing! (304–305). At first unable to gain the attention of the mob, Carteret finally speaks his mind: " 'Gentlemen!' he shouted; 'this is murder, it is madness; it is a disgrace to our city, to our state, to our civilization!' " (305). Whereas Delamere's words earlier sated the mob's lust for blood, Carteret's have the opposite effect. The mob responds, "It *is* a disgrace, and we'll not put up with it a moment longer. Burn 'em out! Hurrah for Major Carteret, the champion of 'white supremacy'! Three cheers for the Morning Chronicle and 'no nigger domination!' " (305, Chesnutt's emphasis). With this response, Chesnutt demonstrates the short-circuit between Carteret's words and their effect within the social reality. For Carteret, in contrast to the aristocratic Delamere, there is no possibility for an act that would resist the bloody tide of history. Unlike Delamere, Carteret is a master who is no longer a master; in Carteret, the master himself has become a slave. In *Anti-Oedipus*, Deleuze and Guattari describe precisely this transition:

> The generalized slavery of the despotic State at least implied the existence of masters, and an apparatus of antiproduction distinct from the sphere of production. But the bourgeois field of immanence [. . .] institutes an unrivaled slavery, an unprecedented subjugation: there are no longer even any masters, but only slaves commanding other slaves; there is no longer any need to burden the animal from the outside; it shoulders its own burden.[28]

With this loss of the outside, there occurs a loss of the possibility of resistance to the social reality.

The crucial question which *Marrow* raises is this: what accounts for this historical shift in masters—from Delamere to Carteret and the Big Three? The answer lies, as Deleuze and Guattari rightly suggest, in the emergence of a new epoch, typified by Captain McBane. Chesnutt notes that "Captain George McBane had sprung from the poor-white class, to which, even more than to the slaves, the abolition of slavery had opened the door of opportunity" (34). The old social barriers that confined McBane to a lower-class status erode with the end of slavery and its aristocratic structure of society. Name ("Delamere," for instance) loses its power, and capital rises in its wake: McBane "had money enough to buy out half a dozen of these broken-down aristocrats, and money was all-powerful" (82). Because money becomes "all-powerful," it deterritorializes all social barriers, erecting itself as the sole societal determinant of power or social status. In the system of exchange, unlike in the aristocratic system, domination is wholly internal—*there is no outside*. The master, within this system, ceases to occupy a position outside of this circuit of exchange, ceases to be the exception that grounds the entire system, and thus ceases to be able to realize his desire in an action.

McBane's justifications for the November massacre also indicate the contours of this ideological transition. Unlike Carteret and Belmont, McBane has no desire to couch the actions of the Big Three in euphemism. Whenever he spots an opportunity for white "vengeance," McBane's position is quite clear: "I say lynch the nigger" (86), or "I say, burn the nigger" (182). His justifications are equally simple; he tells Carteret and Belmont, "We may as well be honest about this thing. We are going to put the niggers down because we want to, and think we can; so why waste our time in mere pretense? I'm no hypocrite myself,—if I want a thing I take it, provided I'm strong enough" (81). McBane's "honesty" represents a clear shift in the ideological terrain; far from being something to celebrate—"at least he's honest about it"—this "honesty" indicates a more complex ideological justification than that of Carteret and Belmont, precisely because it resolutely denies its status as ideological (or as "poetry," in Carteret's terms). Immediately before the massacre, the other members of the Big Three come to realize this: "Carteret frowned darkly at this brutal characterization of their motives. It robbed the enterprise of all its poetry, and put a solemn act of revolution upon the plane of a mere vulgar theft of power. Even the general winced" (252–253). Carteret and Belmont are not "wincing" because McBane confronts them with the truth of the upcoming "revolution," but because his ideological justification supplants and undermines theirs. McBane's "survival of the fittest" ideology, though it wants to pass itself off as the bare truth, is still ideology.[29] Lacan makes a similar point about Darwin: "Indeed, Darwin's success seems to derive from the fact that he projected the predations of Victorian society and the economic euphoria that sanctioned for that society the social devastation that it initiated on a planetary scale, and to the fact that it justified its predations on the image of a lassez-faire of the strongest predators in competition for their natural prey."[30] Lacan here links Darwin's acceptance to Britain's global conquests; Darwin's account of nature gives the ultimate sanction to such conquests—they follow the order of nature—so that we can be, as McBane is, "honest" about what we are doing.

Marrow makes perfectly clear (as does Lacan) that this ideology of honesty occasions a brutality far more severe than does Carteret and Belmont's "poetic" version of things. Their need for "poetry" (i.e., the ideology which disguises their brutality) tempers their actions. General Belmont even sounds like Thomas Jefferson on one occasion, when he tells McBane, "in dealing with so fundamental a right as the suffrage we must profess a decent regard for the opinions of even that misguided portion of mankind which may not agree with us" (81). Of course, Belmont does not really believe what he is saying, but—and this is the crucial point—*he acts as if he does.* It is only through action, through what is done, that the individual "is" what he or she is; the action is the concretization of the individual's being.[31] Hence, ideology is important not insofar as it produces illusory beliefs—that is, false consciousness—but insofar as it produces certain actions.[32] Hence, Carteret and Belmont are ideologically incapable of McBane's brutality; they cannot participate in the massacre, because, from their ideological situation, such action is intolerable. Through the character of McBane, *Marrow* illustrates the increased barbarism of the emergent ideology, one that does without "poetry" and deems itself "honest" in its self-understanding, at precisely the point of its greatest dishonesty. McBane's "survival of the fittest" ideology, which justifies his brutality, also serves, through its mechanistic understanding of actions, to eliminate the possibility of an action which is not simply a response to an external cause, that is not simply a reaction. In this way, McBane's predominance in the novel signals, perhaps more than anything else, the beginning of the end of the subject that can continue to think of itself as its own self-cause, as agent in the world.

Lee Ellis, who seems to be one of the more decent white characters in the novel, wholly embodies this loss of agency. Through Ellis, Chesnutt depicts the fecklessness of the white liberal, his inability to act despite his moral opposition to the violence of the Big Three. Chesnutt notes that "Ellis did not believe in the lynch law. He had argued against it, more than once, in private conversation, and had written several editorials against the practice, while in charge of the Morning Chronicle during Major Carteret's absence" (216). Though Ellis opposes the politics of Carteret, he continues to work for him and de facto support the "white revolution." When the Big Three begin to discuss lynching Sandy, Ellis quietly finds something else to do; he "went into another room, where his duty called him" (182). Ellis's opposition to the lynch law and the "white revolution" of the Big Three never manifests itself in his behavior, because Ellis never allows his private feelings about these things to affect fully his public personality (his work, his friendships, his desire for Carteret's niece, etc.).[33] In other words, Ellis never thinks to draw the connection between his job at the Morning Chronicle and the violence of the "race riot." This inability to make connections—unfortunately, the typical failure of the liberal—has ramifications for Ellis's ability to act in the face of the violence when it finally does occur. Because the violence occurs in a separate realm, a "public" realm that does not directly concern him, Ellis confronts the "race riot" only as a spectator and is unable to act. A good liberal, "Ellis had been horror-stricken by the tragedy of the afternoon, the wholly superfluous slaughter of a harmless people" (290); however, he does nothing to stop it. He only sheepishly says to Dr. Miller in the midst of the "riot," "I need not tell you how much I regret this deplorable affair" (291). Ellis's regret, however, doesn't make much difference; it cannot manifest itself in an act because the social reality, which such an act might affect, exists for him as a realm entirely divorced from his own life.[34] For Ellis, there can be no interaction between that realm and the effects of his desire.[35]

Unlike the liberal-minded Ellis, Dr. Miller and Josh Green do not create a false rift between public and private in order to insulate themselves from action; they do not have Ellis's white skin, which makes this separation much easier to sustain. White racism and brutality constantly remind them, to use the old feminist slogan, that "the personal is the political." They understand, as Mr. Watson does upon the beginning of the "riot," that "When the race cry is started in this neck of the woods, friendship, religion, humanity, reason, all shrivel up like dry leaves in a raging furnace" (280). However, though Miller and Green undoubtedly see this connection, they too are unable to act. With Miller, this inability to act is clear. Early in the novel, he warns Green, "You'd better be peaceable and endure a little injustice, rather than run the risk of a sudden and violent death" (110). Miller's advice is always to accommodate rather than to act. Later, as the "riot" rages and a group of men comes to Miller and Mr. Watson for leadership, Watson tells them, "Keep quiet, boys, and trust in God. You won't gain anything by resistance" (282). Miller, who echoes this accommodationism, then justifies it by claiming, "My advice is not heroic, but I think it is wise.[. . .] Our time will come,—the time when we can command respect for our rights; but it is not yet in sight. Give it up, boys, and wait. Good may come of this, after all" (283). Miller clearly desires some kind of "good," but his words indicate that he conceives of no possible connection between any act on his part and the realization of that good. He expects that good, if it comes, will come *to* them, rather than *from* them—thus his insistence that they "wait." Only the Father—God, as Watson says—is capable of an action that will reverse the tenor of the social reality. Miller's lack of action signals his implicit belief in that Father, that classical Master, through whom all possible good comes. He cannot act because he still lives in the shadow of that Father who alone is capable of action.

A similar Father, ironically, also casts a shadow over Josh Green, depriving him also of the act. In light of Green's heroic resistance, such a characterization seems, at best, misleading. However, Green's action is wholly reaction—a reaction grounded in the death of his own father. Green relates to Miller the story of his father's death at the hands of McBane and how he has dedicated his life to vengeance. He says, "dat some day er 'nother I'd kill dat man. I ain't never had no doubt erbout it; it's jus' w'at I'm livin' fer, an' I know I ain' gwine to die till I've done it. Some lives fer one thing an' some fer another, but dat's my job" (111). McBane's murder of Green's father is thus an external cause that wholly conditions Green's resistance to white violence. This resistance is not an act but an effect, a reaction. Because Green's life is completely dedicated to the dead father, he cannot become an agent.

This complete dedication does provide something else; it gives Green total certainty about his action—"I ain't never had no doubt." Green has no doubt because the dead father is the guarantor of the meaning and rightness of his act. This certainty aligns him most emphatically with Miller. Miller refuses to act because he is absolutely certain of the action's failure: "They would kill us in the fight, or they would hang us after-wards,—one way or another, we should be doomed" (282). Green and Miller have no doubt because for neither of them do their actions represent a break in a chain of causality. For Green, a clear causal link exists between an external cause—the dead father—and his actions; for Miller, on the other hand, a chain of causality exists outside of his action—with the white man and God as the absolute cause—and thus his action has, a priori, no possibility of any successful realization. In this way, both characters have total certainty. Certainty is, however, the very thing which makes the act impossible; the act is an act because there is doubt both about its genesis (Green's certainty) and about its result (Miller's certainty).[36] Without this doubt, subject, as a gap in the chain of causality, ceases to be present in the act, which can then be understood mechanistically: a causes b, b causes c, and so on. One only truly acts when one is fundamentally uncertain about the act's cause and effect. This uncertainty is what it means to be a subject, the result of taking up the burden of the act without reliance on a symbolic Father. Green and Miller's certainty (which results in this kind of mechanism) is a clear sign that both still have faith in the symbolic Father; it is also a sign of their flight away from the radical doubt that is constitutive of the subject.

In focusing on the "opposition" between Green and Miller, criticism has tended to ignore the one character (other than Mr. Delamere) who does act in the novel—Janet Miller. Recently, Sally Ann Ferguson and William Gleason have brought up the question of Janet Miller's significance in the novel. Ferguson, in fact, sees the primary opposition in the novel as one between Green and Janet—not William—Miller. She states,

> During the novel, the author [. . .] steadily develops Miller, who outgrows her yearning for acceptance by her white half-sister, Olivia Carteret, to emerge racially secure and emotionally inde-

pendent, neither hating nor groveling. More significantly, educated and almost-white, she symbolizes Chesnutt's simplistic vision
and illusory hope for a colorblind and racially harmonious world.[37]

Janet Miller is, for Ferguson, a sign of Chesnutt's racism, his preference
for the light-skinned African-American. William Gleason also criticizes
Chesnutt for his portrait of Janet Miller, seeing her as a sign of Chesnutt's
sexism: "Although educated to be a school teacher, for example, she
declines a career in favor of marriage. When she does appear in the book,
she is primarily seen and not heard. Janet is also secretly ashamed of 'the
heritage of her mother's race [. . .] as part of the taint of slavery.' "[38]

Both of these attacks on Chesnutt's characterization of Miller miss
the import of her action at the end of the novel. She neither "outgrows
her yearning for acceptance" nor remains "secretly ashamed"; instead,
Miller defiantly rejects the name of her Father, which Olivia Carteret
offers her. Ferguson emphasizes the fact that Miller is "almost-white"
and links this fact to Chesnutt's amalgamationist political theory, which,
she says, "implicitly celebrates white skin."[39] In the end, Ferguson levels
a vehement indictment against Chesnutt, arguing that "In his quest to
bring racial peace and a taste of the good life to the light-skinned seg-
ment of the black population, he did not hesitate to sacrifice the interests
of dark-skinned people" and concluding that Chesnutt is "not very different from the white founding fathers of America."[40] What Ferguson
misses, however, is that Janet Miller does not reject her blackness in favor
of her whiteness, but on the contrary, rejects whiteness in favor of re-
maining black.[41] This rejection is, in addition, the most important gesture of the novel, because it signals that Miller has taken up the burden
of subjectivity and agency on herself. In her attempt to save the life of
her son, Olivia Carteret offers Janet Miller what Miller has always wanted:
recognition of their kinship and of her legitimacy within the white world.
Miller, however, in the aftermath of losing her only son, renounces the
name of her white father. Her rejection of the Father's (Samuel Merkell's)
name—"I throw you back your father's name" (329)—sets Miller apart
not only from both her husband and Josh Green (both of whom remain,
as I have suggested above, within the domain of one Father or another)
but also from every other character in the novel.

Through her rejection of Olivia Carteret's offer, Miller overcomes
what has long been her deepest desire—the desire for Carteret's recognition and the Father's name. She realizes that "This, then, was the recognition for which, all her life, she had longed in secret" (327–328). By
rejecting this recognition, Miller takes up a radical position, giving up what

had been her fundamental fantasy. In the gesture of giving up her Father's name, Miller makes possible her own act, an act that is not merely the effect of some external cause, caught in an economy of reaction. It is, like Delamere's act of rescuing Sandy earlier in the novel, a truly aristocratic act, because it takes all responsibility within itself, grounding itself on the gap in the causal chain that is constitutive of subject. Unlike Delamere, however, Miller acts without the Father's guarantee; she has renounced the Father's name, whereas the aristocrat Delamere needs the name, and cannot survive (let alone act) without it. This is what differentiates the aristocratic act from the feminine "No!" The feminine "No!" takes place with an absence of symbolic support, and thus has no avenue for lessening its burden. In the character of Janet Miller, Chesnutt creates his new aristocrat, a character who, by taking all responsibility on herself, is able to break from the economy of the Father.

Miller sends her husband to save Carteret's son. This act itself— "Will . . . go with her" (329)—is the source of much controversy; according to the critical doxa, here is Chesnutt's accommodationism in full force, his belief in "forgiveness of one's enemies" or "the Christian virtue of charity."[42] This standard interpretation misses the thoroughly un-Christian dimension of this act—its aristocratic force. Unlike the typical Christian gesture of charity, this is an act that contains no desire for reward, which is not performed for the (white) Father, and which is not a reactive gesture. Because it is not reactive, Miller's act has no exchange-value, it subverts the circuit of exchange. Miller has given something for nothing, and cannot be repaid (her son remains dead). As Hélène Cixous points out, in the traditional masculine economy "the gift brings in a return. Loss, at the end of a curved line, is turned into its opposite and comes back to [the man] as profit."[43] Hence, this act of giving something for nothing is far from being a paradigmatic gesture of Christian charity. Or, if there is a Christian dimension to what Miller does, it consists in her taking up the full radicality of the commandment to "love one's neighbor as one's self."

As is well known, it is this commandment from which Freud recoiled in *Civilization and Its Discontents,* precisely because he recognized this radical dimension. In response to the commandment, Freud claims, "Not merely is this stranger unworthy of my love; I must honestly confess that he has even more claim to my hostility and even my hatred."[44] This is because, as the behavior of Olivia Carteret throughout *The Marrow of Tradition* bears out, "if he can satisfy any sort of desire by it, he thinks nothing of jeering at me, insulting me, slandering me and showing his superior power; and the more secure he feels and the more helpless I am, the more certainly I can expect him to behave like this to me."[45] As Lacan has pointed out, what Freud recoils from here is jouissance—the jouissance of the neighbor and his own jouissance (which are, in the last instance, the same thing). According to Lacan, "Every time that Freud stops short in horror at the consequences of the commandment to love one's neighbor, we see evoked the presence of that fundamental evil which dwells within this neighbor. But if that is the case, then it also dwells within me. And what is more of a neighbor to me than this heart within which is that of my *jouissance* and which I don't dare go near?"[46] In approaching this jouissance through taking up the Christian commandment, we transcend the realm of the sensible, the useful, and the exchangeable. And this is precisely what happens with Janet Miller. Her act of love toward her enemy (Olivia Carteret) is an embrace of jouissance and a break from the Father.

Miller's act, because it subverts the circuit of exchange, radically undermines both her own symbolic universe and Olivia Carteret's. Carteret's response—"You do not mean all the cruel things you have said,—ah no! I will see you again, and make you take them back" (329)— demonstrates precisely the rift that Miller occasions. Because it is not a reaction and cannot be compensated for, Miller's act disrupts, throwing Olivia Carteret's universe completely out of joint. In clear contrast, Major Carteret is perfectly able to "understand" William Miller's refusal to save the child: "Miller's refusal to go with him was pure, elemental justice; he could not blame the doctor for his stand. He was indeed conscious of a certain involuntary admiration for a man who held in his hands the power of life and death, and could use it, with strict justice, to avenge his wrongs" (321). On the one hand, William Miller's reaction to Carteret's request for assistance does not disturb Carteret's symbolic universe; Carteret is able to make perfect sense of the refusal. Janet Miller's act, on the other hand, disorients Olivia Carteret because she is unable to make sense of it. Miller helps, and yet she refuses the compensation of her father's name. What is most profoundly disturbing about this final act is that there is no reason—no cause—for it and no clear result, and this reveals the most horrifying dimensions of subjective agency: the one who authentically acts is both wholly responsible for the act and wholly uncertain as to its result. Whatever the final result, Janet Miller has decisively broken from symbolization and momentarily occupied the position of the aristocrat—the outside. In the wake of the aristocratic Father, one can still become an aristocrat—that is, one can still act efficaciously—but only through a complete renunciation of the aristocrat's certainty, through a taking up of the full weight of the feminine "No!"

5

Liberation and Domination

Their Eyes Were Watching God *and* *the Evolution of Capitalism*

It was primarily through recent critical attacks—negative critical reactions—that the traumatic kernel of "The Yellow Wall-paper," *The Awakening*, and *The Marrow of Tradition* became obscured. With Zora Neale Hurston's *Their Eyes Were Watching God,* the case is precisely the opposite. Here, it is the celebration of the novel—especially of the love between Janie and Tea Cake—that covers up its traumatic edge. The current popularity of *Their Eyes* owes much to the poststructuralist flavor of the novel. The primary thrust of recent criticism has accentuated this dimension, seeing bountiful evidence for the novel's deconstructive playfulness in the relationship between Tea Cake and Janie. According to Henry Louis Gates, "figures of play are the dominant repeated figures in the second half of *Their Eyes*," and play "is the irresistible love potion that Tea Cake administers to Janie."[1] Such playfulness is, according to this criticism, the mark of the novel's political importance; it "jostle[s] any vision of the omnipotent power of rational thought."[2] The idea that the political energy of *Their Eyes* lies in its playfulness marks perhaps the clearest disjunction between today's responses to the novel and the reception it received when first published. It is precisely the novel's playfulness that earned it the scorn of several leading African-American intellectuals, including, most significantly, Richard Wright. In his well-known attack, Wright argues that "the sensory sweep of [Hurston's] novel carries no theme, no message, no thought,"[3] that the novel is fundamentally apolitical. For Wright, a novel is political only insofar as it overtly engages racial oppression (which Hurston's, for the most part, does not). It is the contention of contemporary poststructuralist criticism, however, that a novel is politically subversive not merely because of its content, but because of a form that dismantles hierarchies and deconstructs the binary oppositions of rational thought. Sharon Davie, for instance, argues that the playfulness of *Their Eyes* creates a situation where readers "may begin to accept that the master narrative is one of many, that the Master is a relative, and relative to themselves. This realization in turn can be politically useful if it helps people make the boundaries of the inevitable hierarchical categories they live by more porous."[4] For Davie, the radical politics of *Their Eyes* today lies at the exact site—deconstructive playfulness—that Richard Wright once labeled the source of its apoliticalness.

Clearly, some sort of deconstruction occurs through the development of Janie's character, through what Gates calls her "journey from object to subject."[5] This journey begins with Janie caught in the very binary oppositions and hierarchies that poststructuralism works to undo. In the worlds of Nanny, Logan Killicks, and Joe Starks, Janie exists only as an object and is denied her own autonomous voice.[6] Her relationship with Tea Cake, however, marks a change; as Barbara Johnson notes, it "begins a joyous liberation from the rigidities of status, image, and property—one of the most beautiful and convincing love stories in any literature."[7] Unlike her relationships with Logan and Joe, Janie's relationship with Tea Cake is based not on power or domination but on play. It is, according to Cathy Brigham, "comparatively egalitarian and playful."[8] Or, as Davie says, "their relationship [. . .] suggests openness rather than closure."[9] The relationship with Tea Cake liberates Janie from the hierarchies that her former relationships had taken over wholesale from white society. With Tea Cake, Janie is not forced to serve (as with Logan) or put on a pedestal (as with Joe), but she is allowed to participate in life—to play—as an equal. John Lowe emphasizes this aspect of Tea Cake in his reading, pointing out that "Tea Cake wants her to play in every sense of the word, ending the long line of nay-sayers that stretches back to Nanny."[10] It is not insignificant that Tea Cake's first gesture toward Janie is to invite her to *play* checkers, an invitation that profoundly affects Janie: "He set it up and began to show her and she found herself glowing inside. Somebody wanted her to play. Somebody thought it natural for her to play."[11] The feeling of liberation which overcomes Janie here continues throughout her relationship with Tea Cake, a relationship which celebrates play over work, and—seemingly—equality over domination.

When considering the relationship between Tea Cake and Janie in juxtaposition with Janie's previous relationships, it is certainly correct to read *Their Eyes* as an almost textbook example of a "poststructuralist novel." However, two things complicate this reading: first, the relationship between Janie and Tea Cake, while clearly superior to her previous relationships, is not ideal (given the way in which Tea Cake controls Janie), and second, this relationship ends with Janie killing Tea Cake, an act which, in light of Tea Cake's domination, raises questions about the character of their relationship. Both of these factors indicate, I believe, that while the poststructuralist readings of the novel can take us so far, they cannot fully engage the more traumatic and disturbing aspects of the novel. By eliding Tea Cake's domination and Janie's final act (her version of the feminine "No!"), such readings refuse the most radical dimension of the novel by failing to see the significance of Tea Cake's death at Janie's hands.[12]

Their Eyes is, almost everyone agrees, a novel about Janie's progressive liberation, her emergence out of objectivity into subjectivity. Her relationship with Tea Cake is the liberating relationship, the one that seems to allow Janie to emerge fully as a subject. But at the same time, this relationship also extends and strengthens the hold of domination over Janie, because Janie no longer even recognizes the domination as domination.[13] Liberation always includes an element of sustained domination through fostering a reliance on the Other, the one who liberates. Slavoj Žižek makes this point in *Enjoy Your Symptom!*: "'liberation' always implies a reference to the Other *qua* Master: ultimately, nothing liberates as well as a good Master, since 'liberation' consists precisely in our shifting the burden onto the Other/Master."[14]

Liberation is always also a form of submission, which is perhaps what leads Joseph Urgo to write, "paradoxically, Hurston equates submission to Tea Cake with Janie's liberation."[15] Thus, though Tea Cake, in one sense, liberates Janie, he also continues a pattern of domination, which becomes evident in his jealousy, his furtive attempts at control, and his physical abuse. This abuse is important because through it Tea Cake firmly asserts his control over Janie, and in this sense, it is a symptom of their relationship. And because this control continues to exist in the relationship with Tea Cake, Janie must kill him; this act—and not her relationship with Tea Cake itself—is the key moment of the novel. It allows Janie to obtain a momentary freedom, to lose her submission to the Other. She becomes, at this moment, a subject separated from the Other, and hence one that bears the weight of a suffocating freedom. Though Tea Cake is a liberatory force in the novel, he also dominates in a new and more pernicious way than either Logan or Joe, and it is this domination that Janie attempts to move beyond when she shoots him. By tracing the path of Janie's subjectivity from the beginning, the necessity of this act will become clear.

Janie's first two marriages—with Logan and Joe—are clearly relationships of domination. The nature of the domination in each case is, however, somewhat different, though they share a fundamental logic. In fact, as Henry Louis Gates has noticed in *The Signifying Monkey,* Janie's first two marriages are thoroughly bourgeois, characterized by a logic of accumulation and possession: "Killicks owns the only organ 'amongst colored folks'; Joe Starks is a man of 'positions and possessions.' "[16] Though both are clearly invested in the prevailing capitalist ideology, we can see in Logan and Joe the contours of two different kinds of capitalism: the ideologies of competitive and monopoly capitalism respectively. The way in which each character dominates Janie indicates the ideological investment of each. Logan demands work out of Janie. He buys a second mule in order to have her work both in the field and in the kitchen: "Ah needs two mules dis yeah. [. . .] Ah aims tuh run two plows, and dis man Ah'm talkin' 'bout is got uh mule all gentled up so even uh woman kin handle 'im" (26). The idea of the work ethic predominates Logan's consciousness and is the driving force in his domination of Janie. It leads him to demand her obedience. He tells her, "You ain't got no particular place. It's wherever Ah need yuh. Git uh move on yuh, and dat quick" (30). The rationale behind such domination lies in the ideology of competitive capitalism—the Protestant work ethic—which, as Jerome Thornton puts it, sees "the role of a woman [as] synonymous to that of a mule."[17]

By forcing Janie into the role of the mule, Logan shatters Janie's imaginary identification: he desecrates the pear tree, Janie's ideal of love and marriage. This alienation, however, marks Janie's birth as subject, her full entry into the symbolic order. Janie first becomes a subject not with her originary dream of the pear tree but, paradoxically, with its "desecration" by Logan Killicks. Janie's relationship with Logan destroys her romantic conception of love: "She knew now that marriage did not make love. Janie's first dream was dead, so she became a woman" (24). Hurston's suggestion here is quite clear, that it is only through loss—of the dream, in this case—not fulfillment, that Janie begins to develop as a subject.[18] Logan dominates Janie and treats her as a "mule" to be commanded, but this domination is necessary for Janie, because it trig-

gers the sense of loss which is constitutive of subject. To become a
subject, one must be subjected to the symbolic order in which one's
imaginary relation to an object—for Janie, the pear tree—is lost.[19] Without this subjection and loss, there is no subject, because to refuse the loss
is to refuse symbolization itself. In the *Four Fundamental Concepts of
Psycho-analysis,* Lacan emphasizes the necessity of this initial submission
to symbolization, this initial loss, for the subject to emerge: "the subject
is born in so far as the signifier emerges in the field of the Other."[20]
Without the alienation and loss apropos of entry into symbolization, the
initial submission to the domain of the big Other, the subject cannot
appear. As Lacan adds, "There is no subject without, somewhere, *aphanisis*
of the subject, and it is in this alienation, in this fundamental division,
that the dialectic of the subject is established."[21] Janie gains a certain
(sexed) identity—"she became a woman"—only when Nanny thrusts her
into marriage with Logan and subjects Janie's dream to the exigencies of
the Protestant work ethic (which Logan embodies). For Janie, the arrival
of Joe Starks indicates her liberation from Logan and the ideological
force of this work ethic. After leaving Logan, Janie feels a sense of
ecstasy: "What was she losing so much time for? A feeling of newness
and change came over her. [...] From now on until death she was
going to have flower dust and springtime sprinkled over everything. A
bee for her bloom" (31). This is the ecstasy of liberation, but Janie soon
learns that she has been liberated into a new kind of domination.

Joe Starks does not dominate Janie by forcing her to labor (as Logan
does) but by turning her into a thing, transforming her into his commodity. He doesn't allow her to speak for herself and confines her to the
home: "mah wife don't know nothin' 'bout no speech-makin' [...]
She's uh woman and her place is in de home" (40–41). Thus, Janie's
"liberation," though it releases her from the role of the "mule" into
which Logan forced her, becomes, by the same token, an extension of
domination, eliminating some of the freedom of movement she enjoyed
under Logan. Joe's ideological investment, unlike Logan's, has nothing
to do with a work ethic or turning Janie into a "mule"; instead, Joe's
stresses control. Through a tightly organized control, Joe dominates
Janie in a new way, confining her to a particular position—"her place is
in de home"—within a highly organized structure (which he controls).
If Logan, with his emphasis on the Protestant work ethic, exhibits the
consciousness apropos of competitive capitalism, then Joe exhibits the
consciousness apropos of the subsequent epoch—monopoly capitalism.
An emphasis on organization—Joe's mode of being-in-the-world—is the
primary modification of capitalism effected by monopoly capital; this new

model (which supersedes competitive capitalism and "rescues" it) is more efficient than earlier capitalism because it organizes and structures the chaos of competition.[22] As Nikolai Bukharin says in *Imperialism and World Economy,* in the epoch of monopoly capitalism "industry is being moulded to an ever growing degree into one organised system."[23] Rudolf Hilferding puts its logic more plainly: monopoly capital "detests the anarchy of competition and wants organization."[24] Organization is the defining characteristic of monopoly capitalism and its ideology. While this model liberates its subjects from a devotion to work for work's sake, it also imposes a more complex and diffuse domination—the organization of every sector of society.[25] Janie herself evinces this double aspect of the transition. At first, she feels liberated from Logan and proud to be Joe's wife, but after Joe's organization restricts Janie's behavior, Janie senses that this liberation has an aspect of increased domination to it. As Glynis Carr notes, "Jody demands that [Janie] be not a person but a thing."[26] Hurston describes another feeling of loss in Janie: "It must have been the way Joe spoke out without giving her a chance to say anything one way or another that took the bloom off of things" (41). Joe's need to order everything justifies the severe restrictions he places on Janie's behavior: not allowing her to speak in public, forcing her to keep her hair up, keeping her from the mule's funeral, and not permitting her to join in the "signifying" on the porch of the store. All of these restrictions emanate from Joe's desire to keep Janie in her proper place within his organization.

This predominant aspect of Joe's character is evident not only in his dealings with Janie but in every dimension of his behavior in Eatonville. When he arrives at Eatonville, what irritates Joe most is the disorder. He tells Janie, "God, they call this a town? Why, 'tain't nothing but a raw place in de woods" (32). Joe sees the necessity of organizing the diffuse elements he encounters at "Eatonville" (even the name is not yet "organized"—"Some say West Maitland and some say Eatonville" [34]). In his discussion of monopoly capitalism in *Imperialism, the Highest Stage of Capitalism,* Lenin describes an analogous process: as competitive capitalism changes into monopoly capitalism, "scattered capitalists are transformed into a single collective capitalist."[27] In "Eatonville," there aren't, of course, "scattered capitalists," but there are diffuse elements which Joe organizes, just as the monopoly does, around a coherent center (himself). This is not to say that Joe *represents* monopoly capitalism (any more than Logan represents competitive or liberal capitalism), but that his subjectivity is structured by its logic. It is thus not surprising that Joe's first actions involve an attempt to effect a centered organization. He tells the people of Eatonville that "everything is got tuh have uh center and uh heart to it, and uh town ain't no different from nowhere else" (38). In this way, Joe justifies building his store as the town meeting place and insisting that the town have a mayor (which, not coincidentally, turns out to be him). Through the character of Joe, Hurston presents the ideological form of domination endemic to monopoly capitalism: a totalized whole organized around a legitimating and controlling center.

Hurston's novel shows clearly that Joe, while he does provide liberation of a sort from the domination of Logan, further confines Janie and creates a new kind of domination. The other characters in the novel feel this domination as well:

> There was something about Joe Starks that cowed the town. It was not because of physical fear. He was no fist fighter. His bulk was not even imposing as men go. Neither was it because he was more literate than the rest. Something else made men give way before him. He had a bow-down command in his face, and every step he took made the thing more tangible. (44)

There is something tautological about the phenomenon Hurston describes here; according to this description, Joe becomes an authority in Eatonville because . . . he is an authority. That is, the people in the town obey Joe for only one reason: he acts as if he is to be obeyed. Joe's power does not come from a tangible quality—strength, intelligence, and so on—but from the appearance of authority and a corresponding willingness to obey, to bow before authority, among the people of Eatonville. Hurston describes the dynamics of Joe's authority further: "The town had a basketful of feelings good and bad about Joe's positions and possessions, but none had the temerity to challenge him. They bowed down to him rather, because he was all of these things, and then again he was all of these things because the town bowed down" (47). Joe's authority, his power over the town and over Janie, does not exist in itself; it exists only insofar as they invest him with this authority, insofar as they recognize his authority.[28]

In this way, Joe's power corresponds precisely to that of the symbolic Father in Lacanian psychoanalysis: his power is thoroughly phallic.[29] Joe has this phallic power only insofar as everyone invests him with it; like the Father, he is impotent, and the obedience of the town—like all obedience to the Father—serves to cover over this impotence. As Slavoj Žižek says in *Looking Awry,* "The subjects think they treat a certain person as a king because he is already in himself a king, while in reality this person is king only insofar as the subjects treat him as one."[30] And in *Enjoy Your Symptom!*, he adds,

> When authority is backed up by an immediate physical compul-
> sion, what we are dealing with is not authority proper (i.e.,
> symbolic authority), but simply an agency of brute force: author-
> ity proper is at its most radical level always *powerless*, it is a
> certain "call" which "cannot effectively force us into anything,"
> and yet, by a kind of inner compulsion, we feel obliged to follow
> it unconditionally.[31]

The phallus, in other words, is literally powerless, an empty—and impotent—signifier which has authority only through the obedience of others.
Phallic authority, however, rests on the nonacknowledgment of this—the
belief that the Father has some Thing that constitutes his authority and
thus demands obedience. If the illusion of the phallus is destroyed, then
the Father completely loses his authority, since this authority exists only
through the illusion and is nothing without it.[32] It is not coincidental,
then, that Janie begins to free herself from Joe's domination by proclaiming Joe's impotence, by telling the town that Joe doesn't have what
it takes.

Fed up with Joe's constant criticisms and comments about her physical appearance, Janie finally responds publicly to Joe in the store, the
center of his authority. She tells him, "You big-bellies round here and
put out a lot of brag, but 'tain't nothin' to it but yo' big voice. Humph!
Talkin' 'bout *me* lookin' old! When you pull down yo' britches, you look
lak de change uh life" (75, Hurston's emphasis). By revealing Joe's
impotence in this way, Janie completely destroys his authority in Eatonville.
All of Joe's symbolic authority evaporates with this one sentence. Hurston
details this destruction at length:

> [. . .] she had cast down his empty armor before men and they
> had laughed, would keep on laughing. When he paraded his
> possessions hereafter, they would not consider the two together.
> They'd look with envy at the things and pity the man that
> owned them. When he sat in judgment it would be the same.
> Dave and Lum and Jim wouldn't change place with him. For
> what can excuse a man in the eyes of other men for lack of
> strength? Raggedy-behind squirts of sixteen and seventeen would
> be giving him their merciless pity out of their eyes while their

mouths said something humble. There was nothing to do in life anymore. Ambition was useless. (75–76)

Because Joe's authority had its basis in illusion all along, when Janie strips this illusion away the authority itself evaporates. By destroying Joe's authority as she does, Janie also deconstructs his entire ideological investment and the system of domination to which it corresponds.

Joe's domination, like that of monopoly capitalism, exerts control through organizing disparate elements into a coherent whole. This organization structures itself around a stable and *substantial* center, which in Joe's case is Joe himself (and his phallus). This center provides the unifying force for the entire organization, and it can provide this only if it has—or, more precisely, seems to have—a substantial existence. That is, all of the disparate elements within the organized whole must believe in the substantiality of the center in order for it to serve as what Lacan calls the quilting point, the element within a structure which guarantees the meaning of all the other elements in the structure.[33] Herein consists the radicality of Janie's exposing of Joe's impotence: by revealing that the center has no substance, that it is impotent, Janie deconstructs the hierarchy of domination endemic to the epoch of monopoly capitalism. The organization, the manifestation of this power structure, loses its substantiality without the stabilizing force of the phallic center.[34] Through Janie's act, Hurston thus points the way out of the phallocentric logic of the organizational structure of domination, and it seems valid, at this point, to proclaim this a poststructuralist novel, given that it is through an act of deconstruction, perhaps the poststructuralist gesture par excellence, that Janie destroys this type of domination. The deconstruction of Joe, however, does not mark the end of the novel. And those who would see it as such—that is, who would proclaim deconstructivist logic as the end point of the novel—must overlook the domination that inheres even in Tea Cake.

Like Joe, Tea Cake appears, in the first instance, to be a purely liberating force in Janie's life. Jerome E. Thornton sees a "unity" in their relationship, which "is symbolized by the way in which Janie both shares in the fun times of her man and community and works along side Tea Cake in the bean fields."[35] It is clear, from Tea Cake's treatment of Janie, that he is not Joe Starks. But perhaps Tea Cake, again like Joe, appears liberatory at first and then, in a way Janie (and maybe even Hurston herself) is not conscious of, actually inaugurates a new kind of domination, significantly different from the organized domination of Joe Starks.

Tea Cake's domination, if that is what it is, certainly differs in appearance from Joe's. In fact, it seems at first as if Tea Cake represents pure liberation from the organized structure of Joe's domination without then imposing his own form on Janie. Janie directly opposes Tea Cake to various capitalist forms of domination. Janie tells Phoeby that "Tea Cake ain't no Jody Starks" and that their relationship "ain't no *business proposition,* and no race after *property* and *titles.* Dis is uh love game. Ah done lived Grandma's way, now I means tuh live mine" (108, my emphasis). In contrast to Joe's constant emphasis on using Janie to establish his own importance and on keeping Janie in a preestablished place, Tea Cake liberates Janie from the confines of a tightly organized economy. This is evident not only when Tea Cake invites Janie to play checkers, but also, perhaps most clearly, in the move he proposes to her. Whereas Joe takes Janie from the country—the periphery—into (what would become) the organized structure of a city—the center—Tea Cake takes her from the city to the "muck." In describing the muck to Janie, Tea Cake tells her, "Folks don't do nothin' down dere but make money and fun and foolishness. We must go dere" (122). Hurston is clear about the effect on Janie: "He drifted off to sleep and Janie looked down on him and felt a self-crushing love. So her soul crawled out from its hiding place" (122). The prospect of "fun and foolishness," a prospect which Tea Cake will help her to realize, liberates Janie from the tyranny of Joe's restrictive organizational structure, and this liberation indicates a new epoch in her life.

In this liberation, however, just as in Joe's liberation, there is also a reverse side, a side of domination. This domination appears most explicitly in Tea Cake's jealousy and subsequent abuse of Janie. Hurston notes,

> When Mrs. Turner's brother came and she brought him over to be introduced, Tea Cake had a brainstorm. Before the week was over he had whipped Janie. Not because her behavior justified his jealousy, but it relieved that awful fear inside him. Being able to whip her reassured him in possession. No brutal beating at all. He just slapped her around a bit to show he was boss. (140)

Just like Joe Starks, Tea Cake must be certain of his relation of domination vis-à-vis Janie, that he is "boss." He whips Janie to demonstrate this domination to Mrs. Turner: "Ah jus' let her see dat Ah got control" (141). Although Tea Cake dominates in a new way, he does continue to dominate. Tea Cake's transformation after he contracts rabies, viewed in the aftermath of his earlier jealous rage, becomes symptomatic rather than anomalous. As Thomas Cassidy points out, "Tea Cake's transformation after the dog bite does not seem to be the result of a totally foreign element invading his psyche as much as an acceleration of forces already evident in his personality before the storm. The jealous violence of the mad Tea Cake is prefigured by the jealous violence of the Tea Cake who slaps Janie around."[36] In other words, after the dog bite, Tea Cake becomes *explicitly* what he already was *implicitly*. The bite of the rabid dog is not the cause of this transformation—as the common sense interpretation would have it—but the completely contingent moment that provided the opportunity for Tea Cake to become what he already was.[37] Cassidy rightly claims that "Tea Cake's character change after the storm is little more than an intensification of the growing jealousy which he had been feeling before the storm."[38] This growing jealousy—and its ultimate threat of lethal violence toward Janie—suggests that Tea Cake, while certainly a liberating figure in one sense, also brings to Janie a new kind of domination, which is one with his mode of liberation.[39]

If Janie's relationship with Joe Starks corresponds to the ideology of monopoly capitalism, then her relationship with Tea Cake clearly breaks from this ideology. Whereas Joe confined Janie within a tightly organized system with firm laws and directions, Tea Cake allows her spirit to blossom. Janie herself says, "Tea Cake ain't no Jody Starks" (108). However, this liberation corresponds exactly to a further ideological investment, apropos of Tea Cake—an investment, that is, in the ideology of late, or global, capitalism. Unlike the ideology of monopoly capitalism, this ideological structure is not tightly organized around a stable center, but is dispersed and fragmented, demanding not work or organization, but enjoyment. This is the epoch of the "pathological narcissist," a mode of subjectivity which eschews the work ethic and rigid organization of earlier times, and devotes itself entirely to immediate gratification. In *The Culture of Narcissism,* Christopher Lasch offers this description: "Acquisitive in the sense that his cravings have no limits, [the new narcissist] does not accumulate goods and provisions against the future, in the manner of the acquisitive individualist of nineteenth-century political economy, but demands immediate gratification and lives in a state of restless, perpetually unsatisfied desire."[40] In the spirit of the pathological narcissist, Tea Cake does not pursue Janie because he hopes to possess her fortune, but when he discovers her hidden two-hundred dollars, he spends it all on a party, because "he was excited and felt like letting folks know who he was" (117). Though Tea Cake has no designs on stealing Janie's fortune, when he sees her hidden money, he takes it "out of curiosity," and after he takes it, his only thoughts are his own "immediate gratification" and the image he can project of himself, rather than a concern for what Janie might think about his (and the money's) absence. In this way, Tea Cake both acts out the role of the pathological narcissist and molds Janie into that role. Thus, Tea Cake dominates Janie not merely through control or violence but through the new imperative he brings to her: Enjoy![41]

Though Tea Cake wins the money back through gambling, this incident furthers Janie's dependence on him by exacerbating the self-doubt that she already feels.[42] Doubt has plagued Janie from the beginning of her relationship with Tea Cake; after their first night together, Tea Cake leaves for work and doesn't return, sparking doubt in Janie:

> In the cool of the afternoon the fiend from hell specially sent to lovers arrived at Janie's ear. Doubt. All the fears that circumstance could provide and the heart feel, attacked her on every side. If only Tea Cake would make her certain! He did not return that night nor the next and so she plunged into the abyss and descended to the ninth darkness where light has never been. (103)

Similarly, after Tea Cake takes the money and throws a party, doubt overcomes Janie, who begins to compare herself to Annie Tyler, another wealthy widow who lost all of her money to an opportunistic young lover. Though in both cases Tea Cake returns and professes his uninterrupted love for Janie, the effect of these absences—and the doubt they engender—is to make Janie all the more devoted to Tea Cake and more susceptible to his control. In the same way, according to Lasch, "modern advertising seeks to promote not so much self-indulgence as self-doubt. It seeks to create needs, not to fulfill them; to generate new anxieties instead of allaying old ones."[43] Thus, in creating a feeling of "self-doubt" in Janie, Tea Cake works on her just as contemporary ideology works on the consumer, making her more and more insecure, forging a deep need for a cure for that insecurity. And in the case of Janie (as in the case with most subjects of late capitalism), the cure is love.

Love, however, is not, as one would suspect, a way of transcending pathological narcissism, but rather the primary manifestation of it. Love has what Lacan calls a "fundamentally narcissistic structure," because the formation of the ego in the imaginary relation coincides with the formation of the love object. The love object has a central role in constituting the ego as a satisfying image—in constituting the ideal ego. In one's first experience of love, one loves that object which satisfies one's own ego;

the first object choice derives from this ego satisfaction. In later love relations, one chooses love objects based on their ability to recreate this originary ego satisfaction, which is why to love is always to love one's own ego. In his *Seminar I*, Lacan says, "It is one's own ego that one loves in love, one's own ego made real on the imaginary level."[44] Love flourishes in the age of the pathological narcissist, because, by multiplying the importance of love, the pathological narcissist also multiplies the importance of his or her own ego. This elevation of the importance of the ego fails, however, to erase feelings of self-doubt, the kind that overtake Janie during moments of her relationship with Tea Cake. Even at the height of their love, Janie has gnawing suspicions about Tea Cake's fidelity, seeing him stray away with Nunkie (130–131). Furthermore, Janie remains wholly dependent on Tea Cake and their love relation, despite the way in which their love has elevated her ego. Rather than freeing Janie from domination, her love for Tea Cake moves domination to a new level—one at which Janie herself is invested in that which dominates her.

Not coincidentally, the key characteristic of the epoch of late capitalism, in contrast to both liberal and monopoly capitalism, is that the dominated are involved in—and complicit with—their own domination to a greater degree than before. In other words, even though a relationship of domination exists within this ideological formation, here one clearly desires one's own domination. Though she endures physical abuse at the hands of Tea Cake, Janie seems convinced herself that it is a sign of his love. This changed relationship between the dominated and their domination is precisely why the theorists of late capitalism keep coming back to the question foregrounded in Deleuze and Guattari's *Anti-Oedipus:* "How could the masses be made to desire their own repression?"[45] Janie's relationship with Tea Cake, which seems to draw strength from his abuse, provides a possible answer in the change it evinces in Janie's psyche. While she was with Joe, Janie developed a distance in response to his domination. In a description of Janie's emerging disillusion with Joe, Hurston notes that "She had an outside and an inside now and suddenly she knew not to mix them" (68). The emergence of a distinction between outside and inside—the formation of a distance from herself—indicates, for one, that Janie is alienated, but it also indicates, precisely because she is alienated, that Janie has some distance from her own domination. In other words, insofar as Janie is alienated in her relationship with Joe, she has some measure of freedom from his control. Alienation implies a distance, distance, in this case, from the site of domination. Even if this distance exists only within Janie's psyche—and even if this distance is only created by the domination itself—it still indicates that part of her escapes Joe's control. It is this distinction between inside and outside, however, which disappears in Janie's relationship with Tea Cake. In this relationship, Janie is no longer alienated from herself but attains a wholeness, a wholeness that destroys the distance that developed in the relationship with Joe. Hurston describes this new feeling as a "self-crushing love" that allows "her soul [to crawl] out from its hiding place" (122). In this way, Janie's distance from herself, the sign of her alienation, vanishes, and her self, as distinct from who she is for Tea Cake, is literally crushed.

But this is what Janie finds so appealing about the relationship with Tea Cake: it liberates her not only from Joe's brand of domination but also from her self. Hence, though it is liberatory, this relationship does not allow Janie to achieve freedom; it represents a flight from the burden of that freedom. As Cassidy points out, "Janie attempts to assimilate her own personhood into the identity of the relationship [with Tea Cake]. But Tea Cake dominates there, and the result is that Janie's identity is obscured."[46] Janie and Tea Cake's relationship provides a respite from certain existential recognitions. As Tea Cake tells Janie, "You'se something tuh make uh man forgit tuh git old and forgit tuh die" (132). Janie, too, is able to forget, in the midst of a "self-crushing love." However, the price for forgetting, the price of being liberated from anxiety, is the possibility of freedom. In her relationship with Tea Cake, Janie loses the inside/outside distinction that had developed with Joe. Though Tea Cake calls Janie's soul from its hiding place, though he allows her to realize herself completely for the first time, he also, in this very gesture, destroys Janie's subjectivity—thus Janie feels this love to be "self-crushing." This is the paradox that Hurston develops: once Janie achieves complete selfhood through her relationship with Tea Cake, she loses her self, because this "self" exists only insofar as it fails to be fully constituted. Hence, Janie's relationship with Tea Cake marks the "death of the subject" within Hurston's novel—thus the popularity of this relationship among a poststructuralist readership. Without the inside/outside distinction developed in her earlier relationships and with the realization of her self-identity, Janie dies as a subject just as she becomes one; she loses the alienation, the sense of being out of place, the failure which *was* her subjectivity. The realization/death of the subject which occurs through the relationship with Tea Cake is, on one level, a liberation, but it is also—and this suggests Hurston's prescience—an extension of domination, because it strips away that one aspect of Janie that did not fit; it takes from Janie her own dissatisfaction.

After being bitten by the rabid dog, Tea Cake expresses the hidden kernel of his relationship with Janie: a violence toward Janie's self, which he fears will escape his control. At this point in the novel, Tea Cake literally attempts to kill Janie, to destroy her self, which leads her to kill him while defending herself. Through this gesture, the act of shooting Tea Cake, Janie allows her self as subject to emerge—not, this time, as a fully realized self, as a unified subject, but as a subject freed from its dependence on the Other. Killing Tea Cake frees Janie from the loss of her self in her "self-crushing love" and points her toward an existence outside of both domination and liberation, an existence not predicated on flight. In this way, the end of Janie's relationship with Tea Cake is far different from the end of her first two relationships. In both of those cases, Janie moved from one form of domination to another; after her relationship with Tea Cake, Janie is left alone. This development allows Janie to be indifferent to the talk of the neighbors—"Let 'em consolate theyselves wid talk" (183)—and to recognize the impossibility of escaping one's self and one's own death. She tells Phoeby, "Two things everybody's got tuh do fuh theyselves. They got tuh go tuh God, and they got tuh find out about livin' fuh theyselves" (183).

Through the act of killing Tea Cake, Janie attempts—albeit unconsciously—to move beyond the mode of subjectivity endemic to late capitalism. During the relationship with Tea Cake, Janie embodied this mode of subjectivity, as she lost her self in her love for Tea Cake. The love relationship provides for Janie, as it does for contemporary subjects, a respite from alienation.[47] Thus, when Janie kills Tea Cake, Hurston points—in a way that she will immediately take back—to an existence beyond the "death of the subject," beyond the mode of subjectivity endemic to late capitalism. This is the moment of Janie's freedom, her "No!" to the domination that had hitherto characterized her existence. Hurston shows Janie coming to a tragic recognition: when Tea Cake is attempting to fire a pistol at her, she recognizes that her love relationship—what has saved her—is precisely what threatens to destroy her. This threat has been present all along, but here Janie recognizes it as such. For a moment, the moment of firing the gun, Janie breaks from the Other, holding the support of her symbolic identity in suspension. However, Janie's break does not conclude the novel. Even after Tea Cake's death, Janie returns to their love relationship, unable to sustain her move beyond it. She realizes, "Of course he wasn't dead. He could never be dead until she herself had finished feeling and thinking" (183). Janie consoles herself here, because she cannot help but do so. Hurston includes the frame story—Janie telling her story to Pheoby—to show the limits of a break from the Other: once we speak this break, we return to the Other's domain. If we return to the social, we must put a recognition of our own freedom into words, and this is to cede it back to the Other. Janie's move back to Tea Cake signals a retreat from the great insight of the novel—that in order to achieve freedom one must destroy that which refuses loss. The problem is that this retreat became inevitable when she sat down to talk to Pheoby (or when Hurston sat down to write the novel).[48] But despite Janie's final retreat, with its earlier insight Hurston's novel points beyond the mode of subjectivity of late capitalism, toward a subjectivity that doesn't attempt to avoid trauma, but attempts to embrace it. The freedom that lies in this subjectivity is precisely the freedom we have seen earlier—in the narrator of "The Yellow Wall-paper," in Edna Pontellier, and in Janet Miller. One only achieves this freedom through the refusal of even those satisfactions—like loving Tea Cake—that provide us the greatest reassurance.

6

Agency and the Traumatic Encounter
Politics after Poststructuralism

The trauma of "The Yellow Wall-paper," *The Awakening, The Marrow of Tradition,* and *Their Eyes Were Watching God* stems from the depiction of a symbolic death. In each case, we see a character give up—or lose—the symbolic support of her identity, and we see what this traumatic moment occasions. It is this trauma—and not necessarily radical politics—that has given these works their disturbing quality. Nonetheless, a certain politics does in fact follow from such a trauma. Or, to put it another way, a grasp of the importance of symbolic death has ramifications for an attempt to theorize subjective agency. Through the act of giving up the symbolic support of their identity, the characters in the four works gain a kind of subjective agency, because they throw their entire symbolic universe into question and put it up for grabs. Such an act, as *Their Eyes Were Watching God* shows most clearly, cannot be sustained—we always fall back into a symbolic universe—and yet it nonetheless has lasting consequences. In the four works themselves, we don't see what these consequences are; we don't see the transformative results of these acts. This absence, however, is not a defect, not something the writers might have "remedied," but precisely the point: when one gives up one's symbolic identity, one never knows what the result will be, as the case of Janet Miller indicates. Her act may, for all we know, make no difference at all or even increase white racism, but whatever the case may be, we cannot know in advance. Such acts aren't calculated, aren't caught up in an economy of exchange, and this is why we don't know where they will

101

lead. They follow from a conception of subjective agency that grasps subjectivity not as the product of narratives of symbolic identity, but as the ultimate failure of those narratives. As such, these works offer an understanding of subjectivity and of political action that involves them in a very contemporary debate.

We exist today in the wake of poststucturalism and the poststructuralist critique of traditional subjectivity. Though "poststructuralism" itself is no longer the critical watchword, the poststructuralist critique of hegemony and the hegemonic subject continues to inform much of the cultural studies movement today. Cultural studies is, in one sense, the attempt to discover and articulate nonhegemonic subjectivities, subjectivities different from the traditional Western subjectivity associated with the Cartesian cogito, the Fichtean ego, or the Hegelian absolute. In contrast, Gilman, Chopin, Chesnutt, and Hurston all remain tied to this traditional subject, finding within it—or within their understanding of it—the source for agency. Their works represent a recovery or reinterpretation of a version of the traditional subject and a challenge to the poststructuralist-informed critiques of that subject.

For the major figures of poststructuralism, invoking subjectivity is, as we know, a dangerous affair, because subjectivity always risks becoming a hegemonic construction, the product of a logic of domination. The unity of this subject, rather than being the source of potential individual freedom or collective agency (as the post-Enlightenment West has historically conceived it), can serve to police and arrest the flux of multiple particularities. Thus, the loss of identity—at least a unified and coherent identity—can be liberatory: it can liberate one from one's oneness. This is what thinkers as distinct as Roland Barthes and Jacques Derrida both find so appealing about writing. Barthes notes approvingly that "writing is that neutral, composite, oblique space where our subject slips away, the negative where all identity is lost."[1] The written text, unlike the spoken word, does not carry with it the illusion of a link to a Voice, an Author, a Subject—to figurations of presence, or to the One.[2] As Derrida famously puts it in *Of Grammatology,* the supposedly "autonomous" speaking subject is always secondary to "an organized field of speech in which the speaking subject vainly seeks a place that is always missing."[3] The subject, for poststructuralism, is not so much dead as secondary, displaced as a presence or as an origin. This displacement opens up play, suggesting that the subject's inability to be present to itself—its incoherency—is opposed to the ideological, which always serves to bring multiplicity under the rubric of the One. Toward the end of *The Order of Things,* Michel Foucault voices this idea: "It is no longer possible to think in our day other than in the void left by man's disappearance. For this void does not create a deficiency; it does not constitute a lacuna that must be filled. It is nothing more, and nothing less, than the unfolding of a space in which it is once more possible to think."[4] The so-called "death of the subject" (i.e., its displacement) opens up new possibilities—theoretical and political—heretofore closed off by the subject's ubiquitousness.

Others, however, have been considerably less optimistic about the political effects of the subject's demise.[5] In his *Discerning the Subject,* Paul Smith claims that "most frequently the attempt to 'decenter the subject' has had as its cost the inability to theorize action."[6] Smith rightly sees here that there are two aspects to subjectivity: one that is subjected or chained to a coherent identity and another that is the basis for agency. While someone—Smith, for instance—might endorse the critique of the subjected subject, one cannot fully deconstruct the subject because then one loses the *other* subject, the subject qua potential agent of social change.[7] The basic question to poststructuralism usually runs something like this: if subject is not a coherent unity, if subject is not an essential identity, then on what basis can groups make collective political claims or individuals demand certain rights? This question, or some variation of it, continues to haunt the Left today. The attempts to mediate this question have been, as one might expect, rather numerous. Henry Louis Gates and Paul Lauter, just to name a couple, have openly attacked poststructuralist theorizing on the subject. As Gates nicely points out, it is ironic that "precisely when we (and other Third World peoples) obtain the complex wherewithal to define our black subjectivity in the republic of Western letters, our theoretical colleagues declare that there ain't no such thing as a subject."[8] Lauter is even less patient with poststructuralist theorizing, calling it "peculiarly pernicious" and claiming, in an obvious rejoinder to Paul de Man, that "revolution is not a linguistic phenomenon."[9]

Others have tried to navigate a middle ground. Diana Fuss, in *Essentially Speaking,* argues for the necessity of adopting essential identities even though we are constantly deconstructing such identities. She attempts, in short, to synthesize the essentialism and constructionism into a politics that alternatively employs both.[10] The problem is this: neither the disavowal of the poststructuralist critique nor the attempt to find a middle ground escape the horizon of the critique itself, because nothing ensures that even the strategic employment of the category of unified subject doesn't repeat a certain hegemonic logic, and result in the *expansion* of domination, even if "subject" is a purely strategic category. In other words, there is nothing to suggest that the political ends that "subjects" work toward are liberatory, nothing to prohibit the nonlinguistic "revolution" Lauter thinks he is advancing from being an expansion of ideology into new areas. This is apparent in Lauter's own project for changes in the literary canon and for new, less exclusive, paradigms of canonicity. Due to the efforts of Lauter and other "subjects," canons have undergone some not insignificant changes. But in the process, marginality has become another market, another commodity. Publishers, bookstores, and universities have *capitalized* on precisely what Lauter has been advocating—structural changes in the literary canon. So-called diversity sells today, but this diversity has had little (positive) impact on the structures of capitalist domination. Hence, the political effects of this type of "agency" are dubious: capitalism, due in part to Lauter's agency, has widened its markets. It has become, as it is wont, more inclusive without undergoing substantive change itself.

In short, ignoring the critique of the subject—or finding it inconvenient—doesn't make that critique go away. Politics must, in some way, account for it. Two political theorists, Ernesto Laclau and Chantal Mouffe, have attempted not only to take it into account, but to make the critique of the subject itself the basis for their conception of subjective agency. Beginning in *Hegemony and Socialist Strategy,* Laclau and Mouffe formulate a theory of Leftist politics that recognizes that "as every subject position is a discursive position, it partakes of the open character of every discourse; consequently the various positions cannot be totally fixed in a closed system of differences."[11] Far from being a condition to lament, however, this openness of subject positions becomes the basis of an open form of political agency:

> The critique of the category of unified subject, and the recognition of the discursive dispersion within which every subject position is constituted, therefore involves something more than the enunciation of a general theoretical position [. . .] This gives us a theoretical terrain on the basis of which *radical and plural democracy* [. . .] finds the first conditions under which it can be apprehended.[12]

"Radical democracy," for Laclau and Mouffe, means that different subject positions (which are discursively constructed and never fully closed) can be united in diverse—and autonomous—political struggles, and that no subject position (such as the "working class") and no site of struggle has absolute priority. Subject position, the agent in and foundation of political struggle, is no longer the transcendental subject, but is the product of certain societal narratives, an effect of symbolization.

Laclau and Mouffe articulate, I believe, the most cogent theorization of political agency that attempts to incorporate, rather than reject, the poststructuralist critique of the subject. Even they, however, fail to escape the part of the critique that supposedly functions as the basis for their theoretical endeavor. This failure stems from the fact that subject position, the ground of agency, remains an effect of symbolization; it is, in other words, a product of the ideological structure that it attempts to contest. Because the site of political agency stems from a position within the symbolic order, this politics remains within the terrain of the symbolic, never moving to the Real. Beginning with the political basis of a discursively produced subject position, Laclau and Mouffe cannot suppose that the results of the agency that they theorize would be, as they suggest, "radical," rather than ideological. Symbolic identity—subject position—is necessarily ideological, because it is a narrative, or a complex of narratives, which is socially produced.[13] The function of the symbol is always conservative, in the sense that it conserves the order that sustains its meaning. As long as one remains within symbolization, one remains within the ideological. This is the circle—the circle of "reappropriation"—which seems omnipresent in contemporary theorizations of the political: what begins as a seemingly radical intervention becomes, in the last instance, an ideological effect; what seemed subversive becomes dominant and popular.

Such subversions and reappropriations are the lifeblood of capitalism. It is the genius of capitalism to always discover in what seems to be the purest subversion a new possibility for its own expansion: the sale of Soviet flags, of X caps, of "Subvert the Dominant Paradigm" bumper stickers, and so forth. Though on the level of content these things espouse a subversion of contemporary capitalism, on the level of form—as marketed commodities—they reinforce operations of capitalism.[14] Formally, capitalism performs its fundamental gesture—reappropriation without transformation. This bears on the question of subjective agency because this "reappropriation without transformation" is exactly what agency seeks to avoid; such a process indicates, in fact, that one's agency has failed, that one really had no agency in the first place. Clearly, reappropriation itself cannot be avoided.[15] But if agency marks a break from symbolization, then reappropriation will not occur without at least the possibility of transformation, without a refiguration of the symbolic order itself. It is precisely this understanding of subjective agency that we see in "The Yellow Wall-paper," *The Awakening, The Marrow of Tradition,* and *Their Eyes Were Watching God.*

These four works depict subjective agency not in the articulation of a narrative of identity—where Laclau and Mouffe locate it—but in the breakdown and failure of such narratives. It is only at this point, at the point where identity loses its symbolic support, that the subject emerges. The subject, in this conception, is a failure, rather than a success, a certain impossibility that haunts symbolization. Thus, while we can only applaud the poststructuralist critique of the symbolized "subject," the subject proper is the result of the failure of our narratives of symbolic identity—our subject positions—to ever become fully present. The subject is the impossibility of subjectivization. It is coming up against this impossibility—and thus uncovering her own fundamental dissatisfaction—that spurs Edna Pontellier toward a break with her symbolic identity. Insofar as symbolic narratives ultimately fail to satisfy, they point Edna in another direction—toward their own failure. And it is here that we discover subjectivity (from which Edna herself, in the last instance, recoils).

One's subjectivity, in this light, isn't simply the sum of various symbolic markers of identity, various narratives of self, but what results when these narratives are stripped away. Clearly, we can see the action of the narrator of "The Yellow Wall-paper" as the attempt to do just this—strip away all the symbolic narratives that the wallpaper itself represents. This is why, at the culmination of the story (after she has stripped away all the wallpaper), the narrator achieves subjectivity and a certain freedom. This freedom, however, is nothing but the freedom of symbolic death itself. At the point of symbolic death, one realizes that one has nothing to lose, because one is no longer invested in a symbolic universe of meaning and value. Here, we no longer "make choices"—choices only exist within the horizon of the symbol—but we can put everything at risk. In accomplishing such a gesture, one does not so much permanently escape symbolization as reorient and transform it. Symbolic death, becoming a subject, is thus what Lacan terms an act, precisely because it has a transformative effect. This act is not symbolic but Real, and thus is a mode of resistance to ideology, because it involves a renunciation of the guarantees of symbolization, the assurances provided by symbolic identities. In contrast to symbolic activity, which remains meaningful within symbolization, this act indicates a break from the ideological. In *The Marrow of Tradition*, Janet Miller provides a concrete instance of it. When she rejects the Name of the (white) Father, she finds herself outside of the world that had hitherto been her home—left without the security of a certain symbolic community. This break is the source of subjective agency in the novel, and it opens up the possibility of political change.

This act is a source of trauma to the social order—and to those invested in its ideology—because it is a refusal of the meaningfulness that ideology provides. Ideology depends on rendering all activity meaning-ful, giving a sense to everything, but the act we have seen depicted in "The Yellow Wall-paper," *The Awakening, The Marrow of Tradition,* and *Their Eyes Were Watching God* is non-sensical. As non-sensical, the act indicates a break in ideology's chain of meaning, a point that ideology cannot account for, and thus it throws its entire symbolic universe into question, making evident the gap in ideology that is typically smoothed over. It is for this reason that the act has a political valence—and why it is perhaps more politically efficacious than the disruption of meaning (and ideology) through play (which is a predominant mode of political activity today). As a political activity, play consists in demonstrating that no meaning, no identity, no ideological determination, is final; we can question and put into play every meaning. But by questioning every meaning within a symbolic universe, play at the same time leaves the whole—the very totality of meaningfulness that ideology constitutes—intact. In this sense, it works within an existing system of symbolization, but it isn't traumatizing to that system as a whole in the way that the act is. Play, in contrast to the act, on a fundamental level, leaves things as they are, or it even makes them worse, as we see with Janie in *Their Eyes Were Watching God.* The playfulness of her relationship with Tea Cake is the very thing that allows her not to see the domination inherent in the liberation he offers her. It is only when she momentarily embraces the horror of her own freedom that Janie breaks the hold that this domination has over her. To free herself, Janie must come face to face with the trauma of an identity without symbolic support.

In this way, like the other three works, *Their Eyes Were Watching God* suggests to us the political importance of embracing trauma. In the act of embracing trauma, we give up the sense of security that ideology provides, the security that is essential to the functioning of ideology. Ideology is incessantly telling us that things, at least on a fundamental level, will remain the same: it says, for instance, that "no matter how much capitalism changes, don't worry, capitalism itself will always be with us, as it always has in the past." Providing such assurances is the chief function of ideology. But trauma gives the lie to such claims of continuity and security, which is why trauma bears on politics. The cru-cial importance of "The Yellow Wall-paper," *The Awakening, The Mar-row of Tradition,* and *Their Eyes Were Watching God* is that they make clear how integral trauma is to the authentic political act.

Notes

Introduction

1. The references here are to Allan Bloom's *The Closing of the American Mind* and Harold Bloom's *The Western Canon,* respectively.

2. John Guillory, *Cultural Capital: The Problem of Literary Canon Formation* (Chicago: University of Chicago Press, 1993), 10.

3. Leslie Marmon Silko, "Language and Literature from a Pueblo Indian Perspective," in *English Literature: Opening Up the Canon,* eds. Leslie A. Fiedler and Houston A. Baker Jr. (Baltimore: Johns Hopkins University Press, 1981), 54.

4. Arnold Krupat, *The Voice in the Margin* (Berkeley: University of California Press, 1989), 170.

5. Gerald Graff, *Beyond the Culture Wars: How Teaching the Conflicts Can Revitalize American Education* (New York: Norton, 1992), 46.

6. Guillory, *Cultural Capital,* 9, his emphasis.

7. Graff, *Beyond the Culture Wars,* 12.

8. Ibid., 33. Graff's very formulation here makes clear that Achebe's novel is important insofar as it helps to broaden not only Graff's cultural awareness but also his understanding of *Heart of Darkness,* the canonical text. Bell hooks points out the problem inherent in this kind of move: it "expand[s] the parameters of cultural production to enable the voice of the non-white Other to be heard by a larger audience even as it [. . .] recoups it for its own use" (bell hooks, *Black Looks* [Boston: South End Press, 1988], 31). For Graff, the other (Achebe) serves to illuminate whiteness (Conrad).

9. Ibid., 119.

10. Ibid., 187.

11. Graff's method for dealing with attacks—inclusion—bears a resemblance to that of capitalism. Capitalism is constantly including ideas and icons germinated

in opposition to it by turning them into commodities. One need look no further than a Che Guevera T-shirt.

12. In *The State and Revolution,* Lenin points out the way in which symbolization—or, to use his term, "canonization"—is one of the means through which the ruling classes diffuse the threats embodied in revolutionaries. The process of canonization transforms revolutionaries from disruptive figures into figures of reconciliation and consolation. He says, "During the lifetime of great revolutionaries, the oppressing classes relentlessly persecute them, and treat their teaching with malicious hostility, the most furious hatred and the most unscrupulous campaign of lies and slanders. After their death, attempts are made to convert them into harmless icons, to canonize them, so to say, and to surround their *names* with a certain halo for the 'consolation' of the oppressed classes and with the object of duping them, while at the same time emasculating the revolutionary doctrine of its content, vulgarizing it and blunting its revolutionary edge" (V. I. Lenin, *The State and Revolution,* in *The Essential Works of Lenin,* ed. Henry M. Christman [New York: Dover, 1966], 272, his emphasis).

13. Joyce Warren, "Introduction: Canons and Canon Fodder," in *The (Other) American Traditions: Nineteenth-Century Women Writers,* ed. Joyce Warren (New Brunswick, NJ: Rutgers University Press, 1993), 2.

14. Carey Kaplan and Ellen Cronan Rose, *The Canon and the Common Reader* (Knoxville: University of Tennessee Press, 1990), 3.

15. Joanne Dobson, "The American Renaissance Reenvisioned," in *The (Other) American Traditions,* ed. Joyce Warren (New Brunswick, NJ: Rutgers University Press, 1993), 165.

16. Jacques Lacan, *The Seminar of Jacques Lacan, Book I: Freud's Papers on Technique, 1953–1954,* trans. John Forrester (New York: Norton, 1988), 245.

17. Though the term "canonical unconscious" may seem strange, it does make sense if we understand the unconscious in the Lacanian sense, as an effect of structure, rather than in the romantic sense, as the "dark side" of the individual. Because the canon is a structure, it, like all structures, can have an unconscious, that is, something that must be repressed in order to constitute it as a totality.

18. Jacques Lacan, *The Four Fundamental Concepts of Psycho-Analysis,* trans. Alan Sheridan (New York: Norton, 1978), 131.

19. Dobson, "American Renaissance Reenvisioned," 165.

20. This effort has not been confined to the interpreting of rediscovered literature, but has proliferated in acts of interpretation everywhere. It has almost become the background in which all interpretation today is invested. I can even offer a bit of personal evidence for its predominance: this project itself began as a critique of the violence of interpretation, as an effort to counter the epistemic violence involved in appropriating the rediscovered works of the new canon.

21. Susan S. Lanser, "Feminist Criticism, 'The Yellow Wall-paper,' and the Politic of Color in America," *Feminist Studies* 15 (1989): 424.

22. Lacan, *Four Fundamental Concepts,* 7–8, his emphasis. Lacan's use of the term "demand" here in conjunction with hermeneutics is not merely coin-

cidental. In the terms of psychoanalysis, demand is always a demand for satisfaction, not for an object. The object is, in fact, utterly indifferent to the demand. In using the term "demand," then, Lacan indicates that despite the claims of hermeneutics about respecting the richness of the text, the text (i.e., the object) is always—because hermeneutics is always a demand—indifferent. This is the paradox at the heart of hermeneutics.

23. We can see in this opposition the contrast between psychoanalysis and deconstruction, despite the fact that few of the critics who embrace the richness of the text would call themselves "deconstructionists."

24. Lacan, *Four Fundamental Concepts*, 7, his emphasis.

Chapter One

1. There is no one place in Freud's work where he explicitly makes this threefold distinction about forgetting. However, we can piece it together from his various discussions. For Freud's most sustained theoretical explanations of forgetting, see chapter seven of *The Interpretation of Dreams* and chapter twelve of *The Psychopathology of Everyday Life*.

2. Sigmund Freud, *Civilization and Its Discontents*, trans. James Strachey (New York: Norton, 1961), 110.

3. Sigmund Freud, *Project for a Scientific Psychology*, in *The Standard Edition of the Complete Psychological Works of Sigmund Freud*, trans. James Strachey, vol. 1 (New York: Norton, 1966), 300.

4. It is this kind of forgetting—the forgetting or exclusion necessary for the constitution of the symbolic order or any of its concepts—which has been the overriding concern of deconstruction. Deconstruction sees the excluded indifferent material as the supplement, that which a given concept must constitute as other in order to define itself as self-identical. The point is, of course, that every concept thus becomes dependent on what it attempts to regard as indifferent to it, and as such this indifferent material is necessary for its self-constitution.

5. Nina Baym, et al., eds., *The Norton Anthology of American Literature*, 3rd ed., vol. 1 (New York: Norton, 1989), xxv, their emphasis.

6. The term "American literature" is another symbolic marker of exclusion that critics have also attacked. In addition to excluding indifferent material, such a symbolic marker works ideologically to congeal a social identity. Nina Baym notes the ideological work which the creation of an "American Literature" effected: "Conservative New England leaders knew all too well that the nation was an artifice and that no single national character undergirded it. And they insisted passionately that peace and progress called for a commonality that, if it did not exist, had at once to be invented. By originating American history in New England and proclaiming the carefully edited New England Puritan as the national type, they hoped to create such a commonality, instilling in all citizens those traits that they thought necessary for the future: self-reliance, self-control,

and acceptance of hierarchy" (Nina Baym, "Early Histories of American Literature," *American Literary History* 1 [1989]: 460). In response to recognitions such as this, the term "American literature" has fallen out of vogue, being replaced either by the plural—"American literatures"—or by "North American literatures."

7. For the definitive example of this formalism, see Cleanth Brooks, *The Well-Wrought Urn: Studies in the Structure of Poetry* (San Diego: Harcourt Brace, 1947). Though Brooks is dealing only with poetry here, the work is exemplary because Brooks so straightforwardly invokes the vaunted New Critical concepts of paradox, ambiguity, and irony in his interpretations.

8. Joyce Warren, "Introduction: Canons and Canon Fodder," in *The (Other) American Traditions: Nineteenth-Century Women Writers,* ed. Joyce Warren (New Brunswick, NJ: Rutgers University Press, 1993), 15. We should hear the echo of Walter Benjamin in Warren's words. It was Benjamin's spirit which provided much of the critical energy for this critique of formalism. The well-known final words of "The Work of Art in the Age of Mechanical Reproduction" clearly identify "apolitical" aestheticism with fascism: "[Humanity's] self-alienation has reached such a degree that it can experience its own destruction as an aesthetic pleasure of the first order. This is the situation of politics which Fascism is rendering aesthetic. Communism responds by politicizing art" (Walter Benjamin, "The Work of Art in the Age of Mechanical Reproduction," in *Illuminations,* trans. Harry Zohn [New York: Schocken, 1968], 242). Today, Benjamin's insight—that there is no purely aesthetic realm isolated from politics—predominates critical discussions. Its sway has made any hints of a pure formalism rather uncomfortable for anyone concerned with not being labeled a "conservative."

9. Even in the midst of his call for a canon based solely on aesthetics, Harold Bloom admits the political conditions—that is, the privilege—which makes his position possible. He confesses that "the institution that sustained me, Yale University, is ineluctably part of an American Establishment, and my sustained meditation upon literature is therefore vulnerable to the most traditional Marxist analyses of class interest. All my passionate proclamations about the isolate selfhood's aesthetic value are necessarily qualified by the reminder that the leisure for meditation must be purchased from the community" (Harold Bloom, *The Western Canon: The Books and the School of the Ages* [New York: Riverhead Books, 1994], 23). Finally, for Bloom, this is not an argument against the aestheticism he calls for, but the very fact of its inclusion within an argument such as Bloom's indicates the degree to which awareness of the political dimension of aesthetics represents the spirit of the age.

10. Cecilia Tichi, "American Literary Studies to the Civil War," in *Redrawing the Boundaries: The Transformation of English and American Literary Studies,* eds. Stephen Greenblatt and Giles Bunn (New York: Modern Language Association of America, 1992), 219.

11. The recent interest in the importance of gender in the life and work of Ernest Hemingway is a good example of this. For instance, see Nancy Comely and Robert Scholes' *Hemingway's Genders* (New Haven, CT: Yale University

Press, 1994) and Debra Moddelmog's *Reading Desire: In Pursuit of Ernest Hemingway* (Ithaca, NY: Cornell University Press, 1999).

12. Sigmund Freud, *The Psychopathology of Everyday Life,* trans. James Strachey (New York: Norton, 1965), 349.

13. Ibid., 349, his emphasis.

14. Jane Tompkins, *Sensational Designs: The Cultural Work of American Fiction 1790–1860* (New York: Oxford University Press, 1985), xi.

15. Ibid., xv–xvi. Tompkins has the virtue of taking this historicism to its most extreme position (and thus fully depicting its logic), when she reveals that "my own embrace of the conventional had led me to value everything that criticism had taught me to despise: the stereotyped character, the sensational plot, the trite phrase" (ibid., xvi).

16. Which is not to say that one cannot discover the unconscious in popular material, only that one cannot discover there what is most important in the unconscious. We can see this kind of distinction in the way Freud treats a parapraxis in contrast with the way he treats, say, a hysterical symptom. In the former case, the unconscious speaks through the disruption of an unimportant function, and in latter, through the disruption of an important function (such as speaking, eating, etc.). Clearly, in both cases the unconscious speaks, but in the case of a parapraxis, what it has to say is not as important. For Freud's discussion of this distinction, see *The Psychopathology of Everyday Life,* 355.

17. Freud, *Project,* 307.

18. Ibid.

19. Sigmund Freud, "Repression," in *The Standard Edition of the Complete Psychological Works of Sigmund Freud,* trans. James Strachey, vol. 14 (New York: Norton, 1966), 147–148, his emphasis.

20. Sigmund Freud, *The Interpretation of Dreams,* trans. James Strachey (New York: Avon, 1965), 651.

21. Freud, "Repression," 151, his emphasis.

22. This power over canonicity drives Paul Lauter's critique of the New Criticism in *Canons and Contexts.* According to Lauter, "New Criticism represented an elitist, if unsystematic, mode of critical dissection and worked with a narrow set of texts amenable to its analytic methods" (Lauter, *Canons and Contexts,* 137).

23. Freud, *Psychopathology,* 177, my emphasis.

24. To say that these four works lead us to the canonical unconscious is not to say that canonical mainstays themselves do not engage the unconscious. In the latter instances, however, the works activate the unconscious internally (i.e., within the text itself), but in relation to the canon and the culture at large, they exist at the level of consciousness, simply because they are revered and are not forgotten. It is in relation to the canon that "The Yellow Wall-paper," *The Awakening, The Marrow of Tradition,* and *Their Eyes Were Watching God* have been unconscious.

25. Sigmund Freud, *Moses and Monotheism,* trans. Katherine Jones (New York: Vintage, 1939), 170.

26. Jacques Lacan, *The Seminar of Jacques Lacan, Book II: The Ego in Freud's Theory and in the Technique of Psychoanalysis,* trans. Sylvana Tomaselli (New York: Norton, 1991), 97.

27. Quoted in Charlotte Perkins Gilman, *The Living of Charlotte Perkins Gilman* (Madison: University of Wisconsin Press, 1991), 119.

28. William Dean Howells, "A Psychological Counter-Current in Recent Fiction," *North American Review* 173 (December 1901): 882.

29. Joseph Breuer and Sigmund Freud, *Studies on Hysteria,* trans. James Strachey (New York: Basic Books, 1955), 40.

30. Lacan, *Seminar I,* 191.

31. Sigmund Freud, "From the History of an Infantile Neurosis," in *Three Case Histories* (New York: Macmillan, 1963), 208.

32. Jacques Lacan, *The Four Fundamental Concepts of Psycho-Analysis,* trans. Alan Sheridan (New York: Norton, 1978), 145, 146.

33. Patricia Okker's call for more published scholarship on Native American literature, for instance, suggests the symbolic nature of the change she seeks. Okker claims, "By teaching *and* writing about these 'new' texts, [. . .] we can move along the process of canonization, so as to fully realize a new and always changing conception of American literature" (Patricia Okker, "Native American Literatures and the Canon: The Case of Zitkala-Sa," in *American Realism and the Canon,* eds. Tom Quirk and Gary Scharnhorst [Newark: University of Delaware Press, 1994], 99, her emphasis). We can also see this concern for constructing a new symbolic order—one more in line with the world today—in Henry Louis Gates's comments on canon change. Gates argues that "to reform core curricula, to account for the comparable eloquence of the African, the Asian, and the Middle Eastern traditions, is to begin to prepare our students for their roles as citizens of a world culture, educated through a truly human notion of 'the humanities,' rather than—as Bennett and Bloom would have it—as guardians at the last frontier outpost of white male Western culture, the Keepers of the Master's Pieces" (Henry Louis Gates Jr., *Loose Canons: Notes on the Culture Wars* [New York: Oxford, 1992], 42). Gates makes clear that recovering what was indifferent to the traditional canon will change the structure of the canon to coincide with a changed world—a new symbolic order.

34. Lauter, *Canon and Contexts,* 40.

35. *The Heath Anthology of American Literature,* advertisement (Lexington, MD: Heath, 1994).

36. Krupat, *The Voice in the Margin,* 161.

37. See, for instance, Jonathan Loesberg's "Deconstruction, Feminist Criticism, and Canon Deformation," in which he claims that "By reconstituting the canon, then, rearranging the works that comprise it, we will automatically be reconstituting the values it preserves in the only way possible" (Jonathan Loesberg, "Deconstruction, Feminist Criticism, and Canon Deformation," *Paragraph* 14 [1991]: 252).

38. In addition, "The Yellow Wall-paper" has become one of the most popular selections in short story anthologies, appearing in over twenty at last count.

39. Patricia Okker points out that anthology editors have increasing power over the process of canonization: "Traditionally scholarship was a prerequisite to canonization. Authors were included in anthologies only after critics began debating their relative worth. Now, however, as anthology editors increasingly strive for diversity, authors, like Zitkala-Sa, are anthologized long before they have been studied by critics and scholars. Once given the sole task of determining consensus, anthology editors are now in a position to introduce texts not only to students but also to teachers and scholars" (Okker, "Native American Literatures," 98).

40. Norman Foerester, et al., eds., *American Poetry and Prose*, 5th ed. (Boston: Houghton Mifflin, 1970), 34.

41. Nina Baym, et al., eds, *The Norton Anthology of American Literature*, 2nd ed., vol. 1 (New York: Norton, 1985), xxx.

42. This emphasis on inclusion and diversity is evident in *every* anthology published today. For instance, the editors of *The Harper American Literature* laud "its commitment to both the excellence and breadth of American literature, its thematic and stylistic range as well as its geographical and ethnic diversity" and stress that they "have worked to extend the conventional boundaries of the American literary tradition" (Donald McQuade, et al., eds., *The Harper American Literature*, 2nd ed., vol. 1 [New York: HarperCollins, 1994], xxviii). Their claim that this commitment to diversity "distinguishes" this anthology from others is completely unfounded, and yet, the fact that the editors see the importance of making such a claim is itself symptomatic.

43. We can also see this change in the prefatory comments made by the editors of Macmillan's *Anthology of American Literature* in 1989. They note, "In 1974 [the date of the previous edition], the contributions of women and minorities lacked the secure recognition with which we regard them now, and the confirmation of that recognition has altered the face of the American Literary canon" (George McMichael, et al., eds., *Anthology of American Literature*, 4th ed., vol. 1 [New York: Macmillan, 1989], vii).

44. *Heath Anthology*, advertisement.

45. Ibid.

46. The aim at total inclusion—that is, total symbolization—is not unrelated to the exigencies of capitalism, not only on the level of its logic, but on a practical level as well. In their introduction to *American Realism and the Canon*, Tom Quirk and Gary Scharnhorst point out, "Surely there is some irony in the fact that the reformation of the canon as it appears in ever more frequent editions of American literature textbooks (sometimes, it is true, motivated by a political agenda) should be so gladly welcomed by capitalist publishers, who in their turn have often become subsidiaries to ever larger entrepreneurial concerns. 'Make it new' has its American corollary: 'Make it obsolete.' Every few years, purportedly in the interests of democratization and social responsibility, our anthologies are revised and updated and their prices increased; the used book

trade, which after all, by virtue of affordability alone, once served a certain democratic function, is cut out of the process" (Tom Quirk and Gary Scharnhorst, Introduction to *American Realism and the Canon,* eds. Tom Quirk and Gary Scharnhorst [Newark: University of Delaware Press, 1994], 17).

47. Kenneth Eble's 1956 essay on *The Awakening* and Sylvia Lyons Render's 1963 doctoral dissertation on Chesnutt's fiction both marked the beginning of renewed interest in each writer.

48. In *Seminar II,* Lacan points out the necessity of going through the symbolic in order to discovery the real: "We have no means of apprehending this real—on any level and not only on that of knowledge—except via the go-between of the symbolic" (Jacques Lacan, *The Seminar of Jacques Lacan, Book II: The Ego in Freud's Theory and in the Technique of Psychoanalysis,* trans. Sylvana Tomaselli [New York: Norton, 1991], 97).

49. Lacan, *Seminar I,* 45. Lacan is following Freud on this point, who says something similar concerning fragments within a dream. As Freud puts it, "a part of a dream that has been rescued from oblivion [. . .] is invariably the most important part; it always lies on the shortest road to the dream's solution and has for that reason been exposed to resistance more than any other part" (Freud, *Interpretation of Dreams,* 557).

50. Freud, *Project,* 359.

51. For Lacan's discussion of these three moments, see Jacques Lacan, "Logical Time and the Assertion of Anticipated Certainty," trans. Bruce Fink and Marc Silver, *Newsletter of the Freudian Field* 2 (1988): 4–22. In his discussion of Poe's "The Purloined Letter," Lacan again employs the schema of the three moments, except that in this case he identifies each moment with a specific position within a triadic structure and with a character in the story who occupies that position. According to Lacan, the story presents us with "three moments, structuring three glances, borne by three subjects, incarnated each time by different characters" (Jacques Lacan, "Seminar on 'The Purloined Letter,'" trans. Jeffrey Mehlman, *The Purloined Poe: Lacan, Derrida, and Psychoanalytic Reading,* eds. John P. Muller and William J. Richardson [Baltimore: Johns Hopkins University Press, 1988], 32).

52. It is, of course, Hegel who has pointed out the barrier that familiarity poses to knowledge. In the *Phenomenology,* he states that "the commonest way in which we deceive either ourselves or others about understanding is by assuming something as familiar, and accepting it on that account; with all its pros and cons, such knowing never gets anywhere, and it knows not why" (G. W. F. Hegel, *The Phenomenology of Spirit,* trans. A. V. Miller [Oxford: Oxford University Press, 1977], 18).

53. This is, Lacan thinks, the homology between the moment for concluding and psychoanalytic interpretation. In the manner of the former, the latter isolates a traumatic point of non-sense—a traumatic Real—within the analysand's narrative of identity.

54. In addition, ego psychology also allows Lacan to identify what is specifically *not* traumatic about Freud's discovery, which is what ego psychology easily assimi-

lates from Freud. For instance, the easy assimilation of Freud's sexual stages of development prompts Lacan to cast doubt on this aspect of Freud's thought.

55. G. W. F. Hegel, *The Philosophy of History*, trans. J. Sibres (New York: Dover, 1956), 313.

56. Elaine R. Hedges, Afterword to Charlotte Perkins Gilman, *The Yellow Wall-paper*, 2nd ed. (New York: Feminist Press, 1996), 39.

57. Ibid., 40.

58. Kenneth Eble, "A Forgotten Novel," in *Kate Chopin: Modern Critical Views*, ed. Harold Bloom (New York: Chelsea House, 1987), 8. This essay is reprinted from *Western Humanities Review* 10 (1956): 261–269.

59. Ibid., 7.

60. J. Noel Heermance, *Charles W. Chesnutt: America's First Great Black Novelist* (Hamden, CT: Archon Books, 1974), 220.

61. Ibid., 220.

62. Alice Walker, "Zora Neale Huston: A Cautionary Tale and a Partisan View," in *In Search of Our Mothers' Gardens* (San Diego: Harcourt Brace Jovanovich, 1984), 86, her emphasis.

63. Ibid., 86.

64. Ibid., 85, her emphasis.

65. We exemplify the attitude of the time for comprehending every day, when we hear something new and say, "Oh yes, that's just like. . . ."

66. Though it is ostensibly a work of Reader Response criticism (rather than New Historicism), Stanley Fish's *Is There a Text in This Class?* is exemplary in its insistence of this claim, perhaps making it one of the unacknowledged progenitors of contemporary New Historicism. According to Fish, subversion is a structural impossibility: "It is because one can neither disrupt the game nor get away from it that there is never a rupture in the practice of literary criticism. Changes are always produced and perceived within the rules of the game, that is, within its stipulations as to what counts as a successful performance, what claims can be made, what procedures will validate or disconfirm them; and even when some of these stipulations are challenged, others must still be in place in order for the challenge to be recognized" (Stanley Fish, *Is There a Text in This Class? The Authority of Interpretive Communities* [Cambridge: Harvard University Press, 1980], 358).

67. Catherine Gallagher, "Marxism and the New Historicism," in *The New Historicism*, ed. H. Aram Veeser (New York: Routledge, 1989), 42.

68. Julie Bates Dock, "The Legend of 'The Yellow Wall-paper,'" in *Charlotte Perkins Gilman's "The Yellow Wall-paper" and the History of Its Publication and Reception: A Critical Edition and Documentary Casebook*, ed. Julie Bates Dock (University Park, PA: Penn State University Press, 1998), 19.

69. Ibid., 20.

70. Hedges, "Afterword to Charlotte Perkins Gilman," 41.

71. Katherine Kearns, "The Nullification of Edna Pontellier," *American Literature* 63 (1991): 62.

72. Ibid., 73.

73. Ibid., 77.

74. William Gleason, "Voices at the Nadir: Charles Chesnutt and David Bryant Fulton," *American Literary Realism, 1870–1910* 24 (1992): 39–40.

75. Ibid., 32.

76. Ibid., 34.

77. Ibid., 37.

78. Ibid.

79. Henry Louis Gates Jr., *The Signifying Monkey: A Theory of African-American Literary Criticism* (Oxford: Oxford University Press, 1988), 214.

80. Ibid., 216.

81. Lacan, *Four Fundamental Concepts,* 250, his emphasis.

82. Though the feminine "No!" is a rejection of all symbolic support for one's subjectivity, it is not therefore a rejection of subjectivity itself. Which is to say, it should be distinguished from the so-called death of the self. Whereas the "death of the self" implies a loss of the possibility for agency, the feminine "No!" makes possible an agency that can transform symbolic determinations. In rejecting the symbolic support of identity, one discovers a subject without any positive content, a subject capable, to put it in Lacan's terms, of acting in the Real. Lacan's embrace of this conception of the subject separates him from what is known as poststructuralism. For more on this distinction, see Slavoj Žižek, *The Sublime Object of Ideology* (New York: Verso, 1989).

Chapter Two

1. Fredric Jameson, *The Political Unconscious: Narrative as a Socially Symbolic Act* (Ithaca, NY: Cornell University Press, 1981), 9.

2. For some of the recent historicist readings of the story, see Walter Benn Michaels, *The Gold Standard and the Logic of Naturalism* (Berkeley: University of California Press, 1987); Susan Lanser, "Feminist Criticism, 'The Yellow Wallpaper,' and the Politics of Color in America," *Feminist Studies* 15 (1989): 415–441; Janice Haney-Peritz, "Monumental Feminism and Literature's Ancestral House: Another Look at 'The Yellow Wall-paper,'" *Women's Studies* 12 (1986): 113–128; Mary Jacobus, "An Unnecessary Maze of Sign-Reading," in *Reading Woman: Essays in Feminist Criticism* (New York: Columbia University Press, 1986), 229–248; Julie Bates Dock, et al., "'But One Expects That': Charlotte Perkins Gilman's 'The Yellow Wall-paper' and the Shifting Light of Scholarship," *PMLA* 111 (1996): 52–65; and Wai-Chee Dimock, "Feminism, New Historicism, and the Reader," *American Literature* 63 (1991): 601–622. Wai-Chee Dimock seems at first an exception to the other historicist readings, in that she professes her desire to synthesize the historicist reading and the earlier feminist readings. She argues that "I want to challenge not only their supposed disagreement but also their presumed distinction, to show that the discrete entity imputed to each in fact impoverishes both" (Dimock, "Feminism, New Historicism, and the Reader," 602). First, Dimock, qua New Historicist, traces the link between "The Yellow Wall-paper" and the culture of professionalism and dis-

cusses the power relations implicit in this connection; then, Dimock, qua feminist, notes "a nonidentity between the ideal reader invoked by the story and the actual women reading it," which creates a "dialectical agency," because "professionalism and feminism might be said to be in contact only through the mediated space of a temporal lag" (Dimock, 613, 614). This conception of agency, however, is entirely conformist. The task of the feminist reader becomes one of only "catching up" to the professionalism of the ideal reader, from whom she is distanced by a "temporal lag." Thus, Dimock's synthesis—as syntheses tend to do—strips one side (feminism) of its overriding principle—oppositionality.

3. Michaels, *The Gold Standard*, 27, his emphasis.

4. Dock, "The Legend of 'The Yellow Wall-paper,' " 60.

5. The primary effect of Dock's essay—and the gesture in this direction has become increasingly common—is to say: "we have wrongly thought 'The Yellow Wall-paper' to be something that ideology could not contain and had to exclude or repress, but now we can see that it has been included all along, without our being conscious of it." This consignment of the outside to the status of the mythological, however, fails to see its own performative dimension. In his book on Marx, Jacques Derrida notices a similar thing in all the statements circulating today about the death of Marxism. These statements are exorcisms, according to Derrida, and "effective exorcism pretends to declare the death only in order to put to death. As a coroner might do, it certifies the death but here it is in order to inflict it. This is a familiar tactic. The constative form tends to reassure. The certification is effective. It wants to be and it must be *in effect*. It is *effectively* a matter of a performative" (Jacques Derrida, *Specters of Marx: The State of Debt, the Work of Mourning, and the New International*, trans. Peggy Kamuf [New York: Routledge, 1994], 48, his emphasis). The "purely constative" statement—opposition is mythological—works performatively to bring about mythologizing of opposition that it has declared to be already the state of things. This parallel between statements about the mythology of opposition and the death of Marxism is perhaps not fortuitous. Should we not see the former as the resignation of the Left in the face of the latter?

6. Joan Copjec, *Read My Desire: Lacan Against the Historicists* (Cambridge, MA: The MIT Press, 1994), 9.

7. For Lacan, this is precisely the limit of the symbolic order: its inability to explain creation and individuation. He describes this limit in his *Seminar III*: "There is nevertheless one thing that evades the symbolic tapestry, it's procreation in its essential root—that one being is born from another. In the symbolic order procreation is covered by the order instituted by this succession between beings. But nothing in the symbolic explains the fact of their individuation, the fact that beings come from beings. The entire symbolism declares that creatures don't engender creatures, that a creature is unthinkable without a fundamental creation. In the symbolic nothing explains creation" (Jacques Lacan, *The Seminar of Jacques Lacan, Book III: The Psychoses, 1955–1956*, trans. Russell Grigg [New York: Norton, 1993], 179).

8. Sandra M. Gilbert and Susan Gubar, *The Madwoman in the Attic: The Woman Writer and the Nineteenth-Century Literary Imagination* (New Haven, CT: Yale University Press, 1979), 89, their emphasis.

9. Dock, "The Legend of 'The Yellow: Wall-paper,' " 60.

10. Paula Treichler, for instance, sees the wall-paper as "a metaphor for women's discourse" through which the narrator attempts to escape John's prescriptive discourse (his "sentence") (Paula Treichler, "Escaping the Sentence: Diagnosis and Discourse in 'The Yellow Wall-paper,'" *Tulsa Studies in Women's Literature* 3 [1984]: 61–77). Judith Fetterley calls it "a war between texts" (Judith Fetterley, "Reading about Reading: 'A Jury of Her Peers,' 'The Murderers in the Rue Morgue,' and 'The Yellow Wall-paper,' in *Gender and Reading: Essays on Readers, Texts, and Contexts,* eds. Elizabeth Flynn and Patrocinio Schweikart [Baltimore, MD: Johns Hopkins University Press, 1986], 163). For other views of the story as a conflict of discourses, see, among others, Gilbert and Gubar; Georgia Johnston, "Exploring Lack and Absence in the Body/Text: Charlotte Perkins Gilman Prewriting Irigaray," *Women's Studies* 21 (1992): 75–86; and Catherine Golden, "The Writing of 'The Yellow Wall-paper': A Double Palimpsest," *Studies in American Fiction* 17 (1989): 193–201.

11. Michaels, *The Gold Standard,* 4. Given Michaels's stress on the parallel between the development of capitalism and of the individual subject, it should come as no surprise that the predominant American Marxist, Fredric Jameson, would find much to admire in Michaels's project, despite its wholly anti-Marxist bent and explicit refusal to interrogate the culture it analyzes—"the project of interrogation makes no sense" (Michaels, 27). Though Jameson does attack Michaels on this point, his enthusiasm is not dampened: "Few recent works of American criticism display the interpretive brilliance and intellectual energy of Walter Benn Michaels's *The Gold Standard and the Logic of Naturalism*" (Fredric Jameson, *Postmodernism, or, The Cultural Logic of Late Capitalism* [Durham, NC: Duke University Press, 1991], 181).

12. Charlotte Perkins Gilman, "The Yellow Wall-paper," in *Charlotte Perkins Gilman's "The Yellow Wall-paper" and the History of Its Publication and Reception: A Critical Edition and Documentary Casebook,* ed. Julie Bates Dock (University Park, PA: Pennsylvania State University Press, 1998), 29. Though there are a large number of editions of "The Yellow Wall-paper" that are widely available, I will cite Dock's edition because it is the first (and only) critical edition of the story available. Subsequent references to this edition will be cited parenthetically.

13. In one sense, the "naturalness" of the aristocratic relationship to the land exists only retroactively, after it has been lost. That is, it exists in the mythology of those who live in a world of universalized private property. In another sense, however, there is a concrete difference in the attitude toward property between the precapitalist and the capitalist worlds. Robert Heilbroner illustrates this difference with his colorful example of the precapitalist attitude: "Although land was salable under certain conditions (with many strings attached), it was generally not *for sale*. A medieval nobleman in good standing would no

more have thought of selling his land than the governor of Connecticut would think of selling a few counties to the governor of Rhode Island" (Robert Heilbroner, *The Wordly Philosophers: The Lives, Times and Ideas of the Great Economic Thinkers* [New York: Simon and Schuster, 1992], 28, his emphasis).

14. Karl Marx, *Capital: A Critique of Political Economy, Volume I*, trans. Samuel Moore and Edward Aveling (New York: International Publishers, 1967), 165.

15. The narrator nicely demonstrates the radical kernel of hysterical neurosis, which consists in a refusal to be satisfied with the ideological comforts that satisfy the "normal" subject. As Breuer points out in defending the hysteric against the common charge of "degeneracy" or "weak-mindedness," the hysteric becomes ill simply because she cannot tolerate the "monotonous life and boredom" that normal subjects endure daily without incident (Joseph Breuer and Sigmund Freud, *Studies on Hysteria,* trans. James Strachey [New York: Basic Books, 1955], 242).

16. Michel Foucault, *The Birth of the Clinic: An Archaeology of Medical Perception,* trans. A. M. Sheridan Smith (New York: Vintage, 1973), xiv. John S. Bak interprets John's treatment of the narrator in light of Foucault's ideas on surveillance developed in *Discipline and Punish.* According to Bak, the narrator's room is "not unlike that described by Michel Foucault in *Discipline and Punish* (1975), patterned after Jeremy Bentham's eighteenth-century Panopticon" (John S. Bak, "Escaping the Jaundiced Eye: Foucauldian Panopticism in Charlotte Perkins Gilman's 'The Yellow Wall-paper,'" *Studies in Short Fiction* 31 [1994]: 40). In imprisoning the narrator in this room that resembles a Panopticon, John functions like a "penal officer" (Bak, "Escaping the Jaundiced Eye," 42), perpetuating a constant state of surveillance on the narrator. Though Bak doesn't say as much, the fundamental importance of this connection between the prison and medicine is clear: both work to constitute the individual as a subject (on the model of self-possession) through subjection to a gaze.

17. Jacques Lacan, "Kant with Sade," trans. James B. Swenson Jr., *October* 51 (1989): 68.

18. In this way, Gilman's story makes clear the connections between American ego psychology and the logic of capitalism. The project of strengthening the ego is directly homologous to increasing the worth of one's commodities. The status of the ego is that of a commodity—a thing to be owned—which is why the entirety of Lacanian psychoanalysis is directed against the ego, toward the achievement of a subject without an ego. As he says in his *Seminar II,* "There is never a subject without an ego, a fully realised subject, but that in fact is what one must aim to obtain from the subject in analysis" (Jacques Lacan, *The Seminar of Jacques Lacan, Book II: The Ego in Freud's Theory and in the Technique of Psychoanalysis,* trans. Sylvana Tomaselli [New York: Norton, 1991], 246). This is why in acting against John's prescription for self-control and trying to free her self from the wall-paper, the narrator enacts a project akin to Lacanian psychoanalysis.

19. Though both John and Jennie become interested in what is beneath the wall-paper after the narrator has begun to strip it away, this interest is merely an

expression of what Heidegger terms "curiosity," which is why the narrator so jealously keeps them out of the room. For Heidegger, curiosity, like that exhibited by John and Jennie, "seeks novelty only in order to leap from it anew to another novelty [. . .] curiosity is characterized by a specific way of *not tarrying* alongside what is closest. Consequently it does not seek the leisure of tarrying observantly, but rather seeks restlessness and the excitement of continual novelty and changing encounters. In not tarrying, curiosity is concerned with the possibility of *distraction*" (Martin Heidegger, *Being and Time,* trans. John Macquarrie and Edward Robinson [San Francisco: HarperCollins, 1962], 216, his emphasis). John and Jennie seek out the woman behind the wall-paper because it is a novelty, a new source of distraction. The narrator, on the other hand, seeks out this woman (her self) because she wants to avoid distraction, to "tarry alongside what is closest"—hence her need to keep John and Jennie outside of the room.

20. Jacques Lacan, *The Seminar of Jacques Lacan, Book VII: The Ethics of Pyschoanalysis, 1959–1960,* trans. Dennis Porter (New York: Norton, 1992), 320.

21. The ability of the narrator to turn her attention from her self to the house and then to the wall-paper indicates desire's indifference to its object. What matters is not the object but the path of desire itself.

22. Johnston, "Exploring Lack," 79.

23. Ibid. Because one's subject position, as Johnston conceives it here, is textual—the narrator writes herself into it—it fails to transcend the symbolic order, and hence indicates an abandonment of desire. In addition, because it is wholly symbolic, a textual subject position can't be the site of agency that hopes to challenge the symbolic order.

24. Marx, *Capital,* 77.

25. Ibid.

26. Gilbert and Gubar, 90; Haney-Peritz, 116; Golden, 193. Janice Haney-Peritz also points out the similarity between the yellow wall-paper and the symbolic order. However, she sees the narrator's "identification" with the woman in the wall-paper as an indication that "the register of the narrator's reading and writing begins to shift from the symbolic to the imaginary" (Haney-Peritz, 118). Following from this shift, the narrator's final break from the wall-paper at the end of the story becomes a complete regression into the imaginary and, as is consonant with the imaginary realm, indicative of an attitude of aggression toward the other (John). By focusing on the symbolic-imaginary axis rather than the real-symbolic axis, Haney-Peritz mistakes a Real break from the symbolic order for an imaginary regression. This is clear in the narrator's attitude toward John after her break from the wall-paper: rather than acting aggressively toward him (as Haney-Peritz suggests), the narrator creeps over him as if he weren't there. In the imaginary, where every other is either a rival or a site of identification, this indifference to the other is unthinkable.

27. Jacques Lacan, *Écrits: A Selection,* trans. Alan Sheridan (New York: Norton, 1977), 104.

28. Copjec, *Read My Desire,* 225.

29. For an alternative reading of the yellowness of the wall-paper, see Lanser, 425–436. As Lanser and Mary Jacobus both point out, criticism has almost completely ignored the significance of the adjective in the title of the story.

30. Because Gilman's story inverts the causal relationship within the concept of reification, it effectively bypasses Louis Althusser's critique of the concept as "humanist." For Althusser's sustained critique of humanist Marxism, see Louis Althusser, *For Marx,* trans. Ben Brewster (New York: Verso, 1969).

31. The term "meditation," with all its Cartesian resonances, is the most appropriate term for what the narrator attempts in this story. Though she is no rationalist, she assumes, like Descartes, in her attitude toward the wall-paper, that "some malicious demon of the utmost power and cunning has employed all his energies in order to deceive me" (Rene Descartes, *Meditations on First Philosophy,* trans. John Cottingham [Cambridge: Cambridge University Press, 1986], 15). Her project of peeling back the layers of wall-paper represents a modern variation on the Cartesian theme of "radical doubt."

32. Copjec, *Read My Desire,* 54, her emphasis.

33. The fact that the narrator sees the object of her desire in the yellow wall-paper—"her relentless pursuit of a single meaning on the wall" (Lanser, 420)—is, for Susan Lanser, the indication of a reductive interpretive strategy (which has been reproduced by feminists reading the story). Lanser argues that the wall-paper is an "unreadable text" (Lanser, 420) and "immensely complicated" (Lanser, 421), in which the narrator finds a single meaning—what she desires. Lanser offers us, in effect, a version of the Derridean critique of Hegel: Gilman and Hegel sublate difference, reducing the contradictions and complexities of a rich text into a single story, the story of the subject. Lanser's critique of Gilman misses the mark, however, in its suggestion that what the narrator finds beneath the wall-paper is something substantial. What the narrator finds is a self, but a self bereft of predicates, an empty, unsubstantial self. Discovering the emptiness of one's self, in this sense, amounts to a confession of the failure of the attempt to discover meaning, rather than the triumph of a single meaning over the complexity of the text (which is exactly what occurs in Hegel as well).

34. The vacillations of the narrator demonstrate the ambiguous relation of the subject to her desire. As Lacan points out in the *Ethics* seminar, the subject "does not have a simple and unambiguous relationship to his wish. He rejects it, he censures it, he doesn't want it. Here we encounter the essential dimension of desire—it is always desire in the second degree, desire of desire" (Lacan, *Seminar VII,* 14). The key for the narrator is her ability to desire her desire, rather than to desire to retreat from it.

35. Bruce Fink, *A Clinical Introduction to Lacanian Psychoanalysis: Theory and Technique* (Cambridge, MA: Harvard University Press, 1997), 9. Because the analyst never gives the analysand what she bargains for, Fink argues, psychoanalysis can't be reduced to the provider/client contractual arrangement—I give you this in exchange for that—on which so much therapy is modeled today. Psychoanalysis thwarts the contractual model, insofar as it never gives us what we

go into it expecting. This is an important way in which it is antithetical to the logic of capital and exchange.

36. The narrator is in a similar position to the slave in Hegel's master/slave dialectic. Because the slave experiences "absolute fear," a fear that individualizes, she, unlike the master (who knows no fear and whose consciousness is utterly dependent on the slave), attains "independent self-consciousness" (G. W. F. Hegel, *Phenomenology of Spirit*, trans. A. V. Miller [Oxford: Oxford University Press, 1977], 119).

37. Jeanette King and Pam Morris see the narrator's position at the end of the story as 'the finality of the ideological process" (Jeannette King and Pam Morris, "On Not Reading Between the Lines: Models of Reading in 'The Yellow Wall-paper,'" *Studies in Short Fiction* 26 [1989]: 31). For them, this final act represents the narrator's defeat: "When the woman behind the paper 'gets out,' [. . .] this is an image not of liberation but of the victory of the social ideal" because this woman is the narrator's "conforming self—the creation of social convention" (King and Morris, 31). Such a reading leaves two questions: If the escape from the wall-paper is the triumph of the narrator's "conforming self," why does John faint? And, why, after she escapes from the wall-paper, does the narrator—for the first time in the story—speak of her own name as if it belonged to someone else, a clear sign that she has moved beyond its symbolic mandate?

38. Annette Kolodny, "A Map for Rereading: Or, Gender and the Interpretation of Literary Texts," *New Literary History* 11 (1980): 459.

39. Slavoj Žižek, *Enjoy Your Symptom! Jacques Lacan in Hollywood and Out* (New York: Routledge, 1992), 44, his emphasis.

40. For a thorough summary of the many critical positions on the ending of the story, see Elaine R. Hedges, "'Out at Last'? 'The Yellow Wall-paper' after Two Decades of Feminist Criticism," in *Critical Essays on Charlotte Perkins Gilman*, ed. Joanne B. Karpinski (New York: G. K. Hall, 1992), 222–233.

Chapter Three

1. Katherine Kearns, "The Nullification of Edna Pontellier," *American Literature* 63 (1991): 73.

2. Kate Chopin, *The Awakening* (New York: Bantam, 1981), xxiv. Subsequent references to this edition will be cited parenthetically within the text. Given the large number of editions of *The Awakening,* it has become customary in some critical circles to give citations by chapter, instead of page number. I will follow this custom.

3. Sandra M. Gilbert, "The Second Coming of Aphrodite: Kate Chopin's Fantasy of Desire," *Kenyon Review* 5 (1983): 56.

4. According to Gilbert, Edna cannot find comfort in any of her relationships, "precisely because these entanglements participate in a mutually agreed-upon social reality [. . . and] none is equal to the intensity of what is by now quite clearly Edna's metaphysical desire, the desire that has torn her away from her ordinary life into an extraordinary state where she has become, as Chopin's

original title put it, 'a solitary soul'" (Gilbert, 56). For Gilbert, paradoxically, Edna is "a solitary soul" because she has entered into "an alternative theology, or at least an alternative mythology" (Gilbert, 51). This is the point at which Gilbert's explanation of Edna breaks down, because theology and mythology, as symbolic narratives of identity, are inherently socializing. They belong to the domain of the big Other, rather than that of the subject, which is the point at which the Other fails. This is why theology and mythology can never become subversive: they function as guarantees of a subject's symbolic identity, an identity that derives its meaning from the big Other, a wholly ideological identity.

   5. Elaine Showalter, "Tradition and the Female Talent: *The Awakening* as a Solitary Book," in *New Essays on "The Awakening,"* ed. Wendy Martin (Cambridge, UK: Cambridge University Press, 1988), 51.

   6. Ibid., 51.

   7. Michele A. Birnbaum, " 'Alien Hands': Kate Chopin and the Colonization of Race," *American Literature* 66 (1994): 316.

   8. Andrew Delbanco, "The Half-Life of Edna Pontellier," in *New Essays on "The Awakening,"* ed. Wendy Martin (Cambridge: Cambridge University Press, 1988), 104.

   9. Marilynne Robinson, introduction to *The Awakening*, by Kate Chopin (New York: Bantam, 1988), ix–x. Dorothy Jacobs furthers this position, arguing that "what distinguishes Edna as a modern heroine is her insistence upon development and realization of herself. [. . .] Her daring, her pain, and her recognitions anticipate the existentialists" (Dorothy Jacobs, "*The Awakening:* A Recognition of Confinement," in *Kate Chopin Reconsidered: Beyond the Bayou*, eds., Lynda S. Boren and Sara deSaussure Davis [Baton Rouge: Louisiana State University Press, 1992], 89–90). Jacobs here groups Edna within a whole tradition that stresses the development of selfhood. Wendy Martin sees that the ending of the novel, in a negative sense, confirms this: "Edna Pontellier's struggle for selfhood is doomed because there is little possibility for self-determination for women in a society where legal and economic practice and social custom prohibit female autonomy" (Wendy Martin, introduction to *New Essays on "The Awakening,"* ed. Wendy Martin [Cambridge: Cambridge University Press, 1988], 17). Edna's quest for freedom, a quest, Martin implies, similar to the traditionally male quest (of Huck Finn, of Natty Bumppo, etc.), fails because of societal constraints on women. According to this reading, there is nothing wrong with the quest itself, simply with the society that makes the female version of this quest impossible.

   10. Jean Wyatt's interpretation of Edna is one that does grasp Edna's break from a traditional idea of individuality without, at the same time, eliding this isolation (as Gilbert does). She sees in Edna an individualist alternative to the model of masculine subjectivity. See Jean Wyatt, *Reconstructing Desire: The Role of the Unconscious in Women's Reading and Writing* (Chapel Hill: University of North Carolina Press, 1990).

   11. Slavoj Žižek, " 'I Hear You with My Eyes'; or, The Invisible Master," in *Gaze and Voice as Love Objects*, eds. Renata Salecl and Slavoj Žižek (Durham, NC: Duke University Press, 1996), 109.

12. This is also why Edna becomes increasingly *less* dependent on the racialized or lower-class other as the novel progresses. Having servants is a clear indication of one's dependence on the symbolic order and its authority.

13. Renata Salecl, *(Per)versions of Love and Hate* (New York: Verso, 1998), 63.

14. Slavoj Žižek, "The Sublime Theorist of Slovenia: Peter Canning Interviews Slavoj Žižek," *Art Forum* 31 (1993): 87.

15. Lloyd Daigrepont, "Edna Pontellier and the Myth of Passion," *New Orleans Review* 18, no. 3 (1991): 10.

16. Ibid., 8.

17. Ibid., 10.

18. Ibid., 5.

19. For another implicit condemnation of Edna's hysteria, see Maria Anastasopoulou, "Rites of Passage in Kate Chopin's *The Awakening*," *Southern Literary Journal* 23 (1991): 31–39. Hugh Dawson is also critical of Edna's desire, so critical, in fact, that he includes it as one of the reasons for *The Awakening* being decanonized. Dawson attacks Edna because "satisfying her mood of the moment is [her] single imperative" and because she "hardly anywhere acts from any motive other than her own pleasure" (Hugh Dawson, "Kate Chopin's *The Awakening*: A Dissenting Opinion," *American Literary Realism* 26, no. 2 [1994]: 6). Like all of the characters in the novel, Dawson comes up against Edna's desire, and he recoils.

20. Jacques Lacan, *The Seminar of Jacques Lacan, Book VII: The Ethics of Psychoanalysis, 1959–1960,* trans. Dennis Porter (New York: Norton, 1992), 315.

21. Jacques Lacan, *The Seminar of Jacques Lacan, Book I: Freud's Papers on Technique,* trans. John Forrester (New York: Norton, 1988), 287.

22. Slavoj Žižek, *The Indivisible Remainder: Essays on Schelling and Related Matters,* (New York: Verso, 1996), 163–164.

23. G. W. F. Hegel, *The Phenomenology of Spirit,* trans. A V. Miller (Oxford: Oxford University Press, 1977), 117, his emphasis.

24. It is in the *Ethics* seminar that Lacan offers his famous dictum on the ethics of desire, an ethics opposed to the pressure of the superego and its morality: "the only thing one can be guilty of is giving ground relative to one's desire" (Lacan, *Ethics,* 321).

25. This is one of the many deeply Hegelian moments in the novel: like Hegel's master, Léonce finds himself utterly dependent upon the slave, the object of his authority.

26. As the last chapter pointed out, the narrator of "The Yellow Wallpaper" has a similar effect on her husband and other characters in the novel when she holds fast to her desire.

27. For Birnbaum, this depiction is an indication of the way in which Chopin blames the oppressed for oppression: "Servants and nannies, Chopin implies, are the keepers rather than the victims of traditional Southern society" (Birnbaum, 307). What Birnbaum fails to see is that depicting the presence of servants as reaffirming Edna's symbolic investment in no way puts the blame on the servants

themselves. It shows, rather, *Edna's* investment. Edna's decision to retain one servant—something that Birnbaum rightly objects to—is not something intrinsic to her project in the novel, but the opposite—an indication that she has not yet followed her desire far enough.

28. Showalter, "Tradition and the Female Talent," 51. The whole point is that after experiencing the feeling of absolute dread, Edna is not merely "questioning," but working to change her situation. This is why she is not an exemplar of bourgeois individualism: she does not separate questioning from acting. Every question for her is an act.

29. Chopin's novel is not, of course, an attack on motherhood itself, only insofar as it allows someone like Adèle respite from the anxiety of her own desire.

30. Kearns, "Nullification of Edna Pontellier," 73.

31. The different attitudes of Adèle and Edna toward their husbands also reveal the disparity between their positions. Soon after Edna defies Léonce on the porch, refusing to come in at his command, Adèle hurriedly leaves Edna's cabin because her husband is home alone—and he detests being alone. Adèle dutifully returns to him, and this obedience is all the more marked in light of Edna's recent refusal to obey Léonce.

32. Edna often describes her desire as a "vague anguish" or an "incomprehensible longing." For Cynthia Griffin Wolff, this inability on Edna's part to put her desire into words says something about the society in which she lives—that it gives women no language through which they might articulate their desires. According to Wolff, "Not to speak has an annihilating consequence: [. . .] A 'self' can only mature if one strives to articulate emotions; learning to name one's feelings is an integral component of learning the extent and nature of one's feeling" (Cynthia Griffin Wolff, "Un-Utterable Longing: The Discourse of Feminine Sexuality in *The Awakening*," *Studies in American Literature* 24 [1996]: 12). Wolff here mistakes Edna's attempt to follow her desire for an attempt to become a "mature self." The problem with this position is that naming desire—what Wolff sees as integral to becoming a self—is precisely what eradicates it. Edna only has desire to the extent that she can't say exactly what it is that she wants. Desire is always a question, never an answer.

33. As a curiosity seeker, Adèle evinces a similar attitude toward Edna's desire as we saw in "The Yellow Wall-paper," with John and Jennie in relation the narrator's desire. See chapter 2.

34. For an opposite view, which sees Reisz as the radical force in the novel, see Kathryn Lee Seidel, "Art is an Unnatural Act: Mademoiselle Reisz in *The Awakening*," *Mississippi Quarterly* 46 (1993): 199–214.

35. Martin, introduction, 21. See also Dorothy Jacobs, "*The Awakening*: A Recognition of Confinement," in *Kate Chopin Reconsidered: Beyond the Bayou*, eds, Lynda S. Boren and Sara deSaussure Davis (Baton Rouge: Louisiana State University Press, 1992), 89–90 and Katherine Joslin, "Finding the Self at Home: Chopin's *The Awakening* and Cather's *The Professor's House*," in *Kate Chopin Reconsidered: Beyond the Bayou*, eds, Lynda S. Boren and Sara deSaussure Davis (Baton Rouge: Louisiana State University Press, 1992), 166–179.

36. Lacan, *Ethics*, 230.

37. The role of rebel against convention—a role Reisz relishes—remains, despite the fact that it appears to flout the symbolic order, thoroughly invested in that order. This is because the aim of this rebellion is not a break from the symbolic order, but garnering recognition for the rebellion. And recognition always implies a symbolic investment.

38. This move from desire to drive, according to John Carlos Rowe's insightful essay, indicates Edna's transition to a fundamental kinship with Léonce, insofar as he is a speculative capitalist. Léonce is not a miser, intent on accumulating a fortune through saving; rather, it is, ironically, through spending that Léonce hopes to amass a fortune. In fact, at one point he tells Edna, "The way to become rich is to make money, my dear Edna, not to save it" (xviii). Rowe identifies Léonce with emergent speculative capitalism, which involves the trading of futures to which no tangible object corresponds. In other words, for Léonce, as a speculative capitalist, desire is drive: it has no object that it hopes to obtain, because one's investment always outstrips the goods that are its referent. Desire, as drive, never holds out the hope of attaining fulfillment in its object. Rowe argues that Edna's desire is "in accord with the inflationary laws of this new speculative economy," thus identifying Edna and Léonce in terms of their modes of desiring, but in doing so, Rowe misses one difference between the two (John Carlos Rowe, "The Economics of the Body in Kate Chopin's *The Awakening*," in *Kate Chopin Reconsidered: Beyond the Bayou*, eds, Lynda S. Boren and Sara deSaussure Davis [Baton Rouge: Louisiana State University Press, 1992], 138). Whereas Edna identifies herself with this realization (and thus ends up killing herself), Léonce, good speculative capitalist that he is, maintains a distance from it. He knows that desire doesn't attain its object, but acts as if he doesn't know, insofar as every investment is predicated on the faith that the object does actually exist. Edna, on the other hand, cannot distance herself from desire in this way.

39. Jacques Lacan, *The Four Fundamental Concepts of Psychoanalysis*, trans. Alan Sheridan (New York: Norton, 1978), 243.

40. Lacan insists that nudity is not a natural state, a state beyond the ideological: "Is nudity purely and simply a natural phenomenon? The thing that is particularly exalting about it and significant in its own right is that there is a beyond of nudity that nudity hides" (Lacan, *Ethics*, 227). What Lacan calls here the "beyond of nudity" he would elsewhere call the *objet petit a,* the thing "in you more than you." It is the existence of this beyond of nudity, of course, which eroticizes the nude body and which Edna fails to consider in this effort to strip away the limitations of clothing.

41. The problem with fantasy is that it always and necessarily relies upon a mistaken view of the Other's desire. As Bruce Fink puts it, "The Other's desire, in the guise of object *a,* is never precisely where the analysand thinks it is, or wants it to be in his or her fantasy" (Bruce Fink, *The Lacanian Subject: Between Language and Jouissance* [Princeton: Princeton University Press, 1995], 67).

42. Slavoj Žižek, *The Sublime Object of Ideology* (New York: Verso, 1989), 118, his emphasis.

43. Helen Emmitt, "'Drowned in a Willing Sea': Freedom and Drowning in Eliot, Chopin, and Drabble," *Tulsa Studies in Women's Literature* 12 (1993): 324.

44. Wyatt, *Reconstructing Desire,* 68.

Chapter Four

1. P. Jay Delmar, "The Moral Dilemma in Charles W. Chesnutt's *The Marrow of Tradition*," *American Literary Realism, 1870–1910* 14 (1981): 272.

2. William Gleason, "Voices at the Nadir: Charles Chesnutt and David Bryant Fulton," *American Literary Realism, 1870–1910* 24 (1992): 22.

3. William L. Andrews, *The Literary Career of Charles W. Chesnutt* (Baton Rouge: Louisiana State University Press, 1980), 174, 198.

4. Ibid., 200.

5. Gleason, "Voices at the Nadir," 34.

6. Sally Ann Ferguson, "Chesnutt's Genuine Blacks and Future Americans," *MELUS* 15 (1988): 117.

7. For instance, see John M. Reilly, "The Dilemma in Chesnutt's *The Marrow of Tradition*," *Phylon* 32 (1971): 31–38; Charles Hackenberry, "Meaning and Models: The Uses of Characterization in Chesnutt's *The Marrow of Tradition* and *Mandy Oxendine*," *American Literary Realism, 1870–1910,* 17 (1984): 193–202; Marjorie George and Richard S. Pressman, "Confronting the Shadow: Psycho-Political Repression in Chesnutt's *The Marrow of Tradition*," *Phylon* 48 (1987): 287–298.

8. This is Hegel's fundamental lesson: it is the ability to reflect on itself that alienates humanity from the rest of existence, but it is only through this ability to reflect that we can possibly counter the effects of our alienated existence.

9. Charles W. Chesnutt, *The Marrow of Tradition* (New York: Penguin, 1993), 211. Subsequent references to this edition will be cited parenthetically.

10. It is not difficult to see in the contrast between Delamere and McBane Nietzsche's distinction between a noble and a slave morality. Noble morality is characteristically active, proceeding out of an abundance of itself, while the slave morality is passive or reactive, consumed by *ressentiment.* As Nietzsche says in his *Genealogy of Morals,* "in order to exist, slave morality always needs a hostile external world; it needs, physiologically speaking, external stimuli in order to act at all—its action is fundamentally reaction" (Friedrich Nietzsche, *On the Genealogy of Morals,* trans. Walter Kaufmann and R. J. Hollingdale [New York: Vintage, 1967], 37). Noble morality, in contrast, "develops from a triumphant affirmation of itself" (Nietzsche, *Genealogy,* 36) and hence views the external world as the manifestation of its own agency.

11. Slavoj Žižek, *For they know not what they do: Enjoyment as a political factor* (New York: Verso, 1991), 235.

12. G. W. F. Hegel, *Phenomenology of Spirit,* trans. A. V. Miller (Oxford: Oxford University Press, 1977), 311, his emphasis.

13. Joyce Pettis, "The Literary Imagination and the Historic Event: Chesnutt's Use of History in *The Marrow of Tradition*," *South Atlantic Review* 55 (1990): 40.

14. G. W. F. Hegel, *Philosophy of Right*, trans. T. M. Knox (London: Oxford University Press, 1952), 288.

15. Symbolic authority is always based on a deception—that is, the deception that the authority in itself actually has a substantial existence. This deception deceives both those in authority and those under authority, but it is the deception of the former that is perhaps more important for the functioning of authority. If a figure of symbolic authority ceases to believe in his own authority, he will no longer carry himself like an authority, and those under him will be quickly stripped of their deception as well.

16. Andrews, *Literary Career of Chesnutt*, 201.

17. This is true on another level as well. In both cases when an aristocrat dies in the novel (Samuel Merkell and Mr. Delamere), his literal *will* is suppressed and its realization is thereby short-circuited.

18. Andrews, *Literary Career of Chesnutt*, 202.

19. This is not the only seeming formal deficiency that is crucial to the political import of the novel. Chesnutt seems to "forget" about the relationship between Lee Ellis and Major Carteret's neice Clara—an important plot line at the beginning of the novel—after the "race riot" begins to heat up. However, this "elision" points directly to unimportance of the personal in the face of the political. The fact that the plot line drops out of the novel makes clear that the sentimentality of this relationship no longer has a place in the novelistic world of the "race riot."

20. Hegel's retention of the monarch in the *Philosophy of Right* has, of course, made him the subject of numerous attacks, which have characterized him as a conformist or even a reactionary. Because the constitutional monarch is the endpoint in the *Philosophy of Right*, most see the book as a retreat from the more revolutionary insights of the *Phenomenology*, as the product of the conservatism of middle age and status within the establishment. (Hegel was 51 when the *Philosophy of Right* was published and held a prestigious chair at the University of Berlin.) This reading, however, glosses over Hegel's emphasis on the stupidity of the monarch; it is his or her stupidity or irrationality that allows the *socius* to attain a rational consistency. The best monarch is not the one best qualified for the job, but the one least so, because he or she exhibits the monarch's irrationality in its pure form. Without the point of irrational exception that *is* the monarch, the *socius* loses its rational structure, because its rationality depends on a point of exception to rationality.

21. Hegel, *Philosophy of Right*, 279.

22. Ibid.

23. Ibid.

24. This loss of the aristocrat also gives birth to the lynch mob. As Žižek points out in *Enjoy Your Symptom!*, "The crowd enters the stage when history

is no longer regulated by the texture of symbolic destiny, i.e., when the father's phallic authority is broken" (Slavoj Žižek, *Enjoy Your Symptom! Jacques Lacan In Hollywood and Out* [New York: Routledge, 1992], 20).

25. Chesnutt thus shows the importance of capitalism and its development in making a break from the symbolic order more difficult (and at the same time more necessary). In *Their Eyes Were Watching God*, Hurston takes this motif even further. See the following chapter.

26. The "Big Three's" paranoiac view of the social reality—African Americans are *really* controlling Wellington—is the fullest development of a slave morality, which begins with an antagonistic relationship between self and social reality.

27. In this way, the attitude of the "Big Three" represents an eerie precursor of today's social and political climate. One can attack, say, affirmative action today and have the feeling that one is really fighting against oppression, despite the fact that the targets of this attack clearly do not comprise the oppressive power structure within contemporary American society.

28. Gilles Deleuze and Félix Guattari, *Anti-Oedipus: Capitalism and Schizophrenia*, trans. Robert Hurley, Mark Seem, and H. R. Lane (Minneapolis: University of Minnesota Press, 1983), 254.

29. McBane's gesture of distinguishing between what is ideological ("merely poetry") and what is true is itself, according to Slavoj Žižek, the fundamental *ideological* operation. Žižek points out that "a gesture which draws the line of separation between 'real problems' and 'ideological chimeras' is, from Plato onwards, the very founding gesture of ideology: ideology is by definition self-referential—that is, it always establishes itself by assuming a distance towards (what it denounces as) 'mere ideology'" (Slavoj Žižek, *The Plague of Fantasies* [New York: Verso, 1997], 167).

30. Jacques Lacan, *Ecrits: A Selection*, trans. Alan Sheridan (New York: Norton, 1977), 26.

31. This idea—that one is what one does—is the controlling idea in Hegel's *Phenomenology*. Hegel develops the contradiction of each position he discusses by comparing the action that results from a position to what the position proclaims about itself.

32. In perhaps the most well-known statement in *The German Ideology*, Marx and Engels say, "in all ideology men and their relations appear upside-down as in a *camera obscura*" (Karl Marx and Frederick Engels, *The German Ideology* [Moscow: Progress Publishers, 1976], 42). It no longer makes sense to accept this "false consciousness" definition of "ideology," in an age where the dominant mode of subjectivity is one of cynical distance. Today, everyone knows that, to choose the obvious example, advertisements lie, and yet they remain as effective as ever in selling products. Herbert Marcuse notices this very thing in *One-Dimensional Man*: "It seems unwarranted to assume that the recipients believe, or are made to believe, what they are being told. The new touch of the magic-ritual language rather is that people don't believe it, or don't care, and yet act accordingly. One does not 'believe' the statement of an operational concept but it justifies itself in

action" (Herbert Marcuse, *One-Dimensional Man* [Boston: Beacon Press, 1964], 103). Ideology can thus include cynical distance toward itself within its functioning without disturbing that functioning. In fact, because it provides a feeling of transgression in its subjects, such cynical distance actually allows ideology to operate more smoothly. Ideology is its effects, not the beliefs it produces.

33. This public/private split predominating in Ellis is the mark of a reified consciousness, which Georg Lukács discusses at length in his *History and Class Consciousness*. Coincidentally, Lukács' example of this consciousness is the journalist. He notes, "This phenomenon [of reification] can be seen at its most grotesque in journalism. Here it is precisely subjectivity itself, knowledge, temperament and powers of expression that are reduced to an abstract mechanism functioning autonomously and divorced from both the personality of their 'owner' and from the material and concrete nature of the subject matter in hand. The journalist's 'lack of convictions,' the prostitution of his experiences and beliefs is comprehensible only as the apogee of capitalist reification" (Georg Lukács, *History and Class Consciousness: Studies in Marxist Dialectics,* trans. Rodney Livingstone [Cambridge: MIT Press, 1971], 100). Through this splitting, reification renders agency impossible, because it constitutes a disjunction between what one thinks and how one acts. For Lukács, of course, only the proletariat, as the subject/object of history, could overcome reification and heal this wound.

34. In fact, Ellis's regret, his compassion for Miller, allows him specifically *not* to act. It offers him a consolation—"at least I care"—which relieves him of the burden of actually doing anything to stop the massacre. This is the consistent function of compassion: it replaces action.

35. Ellis is the direct ancestor of today's "apolitical" pathological narcissist, constantly obsessing about romance and "love," and disavowing any interest in the overtly political.

36. Certainty is also the indication that desire is absent. Desire is always a question to the Other—what do you want from me?—and thus is something that we cannot be sure about.

37. Ferguson, "Genuine Blacks and Future Americans," 117.

38. Gleason, "Voices at the Nadir," 37.

39. Ferguson, "Genuine Blacks and Future Americans," 116. Ferguson tries to read *Marrow* through the lens of Chesnutt's essays on "The Future American." While this does effectively explain the novel, this procedure also has the effect of reducing the novel to the essays. Ferguson's method assimilates the complex *(Marrow)* to the simple (the essays), and hence disarms the novel by explaining it. The reverse procedure—explaining the essay through the lens of the novel—has the opposite effect, revealing the complexity of the seemingly simple (the essay). As Sartre says about Flaubert, "We shall not find an embryonic *Madame Bovary* in the correspondence, but we shall greatly clarify the correspondence by means of Madame Bovary" (Jean-Paul Sartre, *Search for a Method,* trans. Hazel E. Barnes [New York: Vintage, 1968], 142).

40. Ferguson, "Genuine Blacks and Future Americans," 118.

41. Chesnutt takes this motif even further in his last two novels, *Paul Marchand, F. M. C.* and *The Quarry* (which were never published). In both novels, a character who has supposed himself black all his life learns that he is "really" white. And in both cases, he rejects the "gift" of white identity and chooses to remain, publicly, African American.

42. Delmar, "Moral Dilemma," 270; Andrews, *Literary Career of Chesnutt,* 200.

43. Hélène Cixous, "Sorties: Out and Out: Attacks/Ways Out/Forays," in Helene Cixous and Catherine Clement, *The Newly Born Woman,* trans. Betsy Wing (Minneapolis: University of Minnesota Press, 1986), 87.

44. Sigmund Freud, *Civilization and Its Discontents,* trans. James Strachey (New York: Norton, 1961), 67.

45. Freud, *Civilization,* 67.

46. Jacques Lacan, *The Seminar of Jacques Lacan, Book VII: The Ethics of Psychoanalysis, 1959–1960,* trans. Dennis Porter (New York: Norton, 1992), 186.

Chapter Five

1. Henry Louis Gates Jr., *The Signifying Monkey: A Theory of African-American Literary Criticism* (New York: Oxford University Press, 1988), 194, 195.

2. Sharon Davie, "Free Mules, Talking Buzzards, and Cracked Plates: The Politics of Dislocation in *Their Eyes Were Watching God,*" *PMLA* 108 (1993): 448.

3. Richard Wright, "Between Laughter and Tears" *New Masses* (Oct. 1937): 25.

4. Davie, "Free Mules," 457.

5. Henry Louis Gates Jr., "Zora Neale Hurston: 'A Negro Way of Saying,'" afterword to *Their Eyes Were Watching God,* by Zora Neale Hurston (New York: Harper and Row, 1990), 187.

6. Since it has emerged as a canonical work, *Their Eyes* has occasioned much discussion about the importance of Janie's voice in the novel (for an account of an early version of this discussion—Robert Stepto and Alice Walker's debate about Janie's voice at the 1979 MLA convention in San Francisco—see Mary Helen Washington, Foreword to *Their Eyes Were Watching God,* by Zora Neale Hurston [New York: Harper and Row, 1990], x–xii). Continuing in this tradition, much recent criticism has tended to see the novel as the progressive development of Janie's voice. Acquiring and developing a voice becomes, in this reading, the method of achieving selfhood. As Maria Racine puts it, "having a voice means owning one's self and living as an independent person who makes her own decisions and determines her own life" (Maria J. Racine, "Voice and Interiority in Zora Neale Hurston's *Their Eyes Were Watching God,*" *African American Review* 28 [1994]: 290). For another view of the development of Janie's voice, see Cathy Brigham, "The Talking Frame of Zora Neale Hurston's

Talking Book: Storytelling as Dialectic in *Their Eyes Were Watching God*," *CLA Journal* 37 (1994): 402–419.

7. Barbara Johnson, *A World of Difference* (Baltimore, MD: Johns Hopkins University Press, 1987), 160.

8. Brigham, "The Talking Frame," 413.

9. Davie, "Free Mules," 454.

10. John Lowe, *Jump at the Sun: Zora Neale Hurston's Cosmic Comedy* (Urbana: University of Illinois Press, 1995), 178.

11. Zora Neale Hurston, *Their Eyes Were Watching God* (New York: Harper and Row, 1990), 91–92. Subsequent references to this edition will be cited parenthetically.

12. Such readings often seem to acknowledge Tea Cake's treatment of Janie, but in effect ignore it, by not allowing it to influence the interpretation of the novel. For instance, Mary Helen Washington rightly has "questions" about the novel's "uncritical depiction of violence toward women" (Washington, Foreword, xiv). The problem is that the "questions" exist outside of Washington's interpretation—which praises the relationship between Janie and Tea Cake—and have no effect on it.

13. Joseph Urgo correctly sees that domination exists in each of Janie's relationships: "The mistake easily made in reading the novel as a progression from bad to mediocre to best mate for Janie is to miss the repetition of treatment Janie receives from each man. Each man seeks domination, each man seeks possession. Each man physically assaults her" (Joseph Urgo, "'The Tune Is the Unity of the Thing': Power and Vulnerability in Zora Neale Hurston's *Their Eyes Were Watching God*," *Southern Literary Journal* 23 [1991]: 52). What Urgo's otherwise insightful point misses is that not only does each successive man in Janie's life continue to dominate her, but that each also expands this domination, precisely because it comes to seem less and less like domination (both to Janie and to many readers of the novel).

14. Slavoj Žižek, *Enjoy Your Symptom! Jacques Lacan In Hollywood and Out* (New York: Routledge, 1992), 59. Liberation, in this sense, is wholly opposed to freedom, which involves giving up the symbolic identity which the Other provides. As Žižek says, "freedom [. . .] is a point at which we find ourselves not only without the other *qua* our neighbor, but without support in the Other itself—as such, it is unbearably suffocating, the very opposite of relief, of 'freedom'" (Žižek, *Enjoy Your Symptom*, 59).

15. Urgo, "Tune Is the Unity," 52.

16. Gates, *Signifying Monkey*, 186.

17. Jerome Thornton, "'Goin' on de Muck': The Paradoxical Journey of the Black American Hero," *CLA Journal* 31 (1988): 264. In *The Protestant Ethic and the Spirit of Capitalism*, Max Weber identifies (what was originally) Christian asceticism with the spirit of capitalism. According to such asceticism, "not leisure and enjoyment, but only activity serves to increase the glory of God, according to the definite manifestations of His will" (Max Weber, *The Protestant Ethic and*

the Spirit of Capitalism, trans. Talcott Parsons [London: Routledge, 1992], 157). The ideology of asceticism has as its archetype the hard-working individual— Logan Killicks. What Weber does not discuss—and what is revealed in Hurston's novel—are the subsequent "spirit(s) of capitalism" which follow in the wake of asceticism.

18. It is Hegel who first conceived of the necessity of an initial loss for the dialectic of the subject to commence. For his well-known discussion of this aspect of Hegel's thought, see Alexandre Kojève, *Introduction to the Reading of Hegel: Lectures on the "Phenomenology of Spirit,"* trans. James H. Nichols Jr. [Ithaca, NY: Cornell University Press, 1969].

19. Lacan defines the symbolic order as the world where objects are lost, where we get the symbol in place of the object.

20. Jacques Lacan, *The Four Fundamental Concepts of Psycho-Analysis,* trans. Alan Sheridan (New York: Norton, 1978), 199.

21. Ibid., 221.

22. The transition from liberal to monopoly capitalism, as Paul Baran and Paul Sweezy note in their *Monopoly Capital,* effects "a shift in the center of gravity from production to sales" (Paul A. Baran and Paul M. Sweezy, *Monopoly Capital: An Essay on the American Economic and Social Order* [New York: Monthly Review Press, 1966], 131). This shift is directly homologous to the change in emphasis from work ethic to organization—and from Logan to Joe. Whereas Logan is only concerned with his own (and Janie's) production, Joe must concern himself with marketing both himself and Janie to others. This is why, though Janie is not forced to work, she must occupy a certain symbolic position, above the interaction of the other citizens of Eatonville.

23. Nikolai Bukharin, *Imperialism and World Economy* (New York: Monthly Review Press, 1937), 51–52.

24. Rudlolf Hilferding, *Finance Capital: A Study of the Latest Phase of Capitalist Development,* trans. Morris Watnick and Sam Gordon (London: Routledge, 1981), 334.

25. Because monopoly capitalism is oriented ideologically around organization, the mode of subjectivity which corresponds to it is not the "autonomous" individual devoted to the work ethic, but the "organization man," devoted to being accepted and loved by the group—following its rules—rather than differentiating him/herself.

26. Glynis Carr, "Storytelling as *Bildung* in Zora Neale Hurston's *Their Eyes Were Watching God,*" *CLA Journal* 31 (1987): 197.

27. V. I. Lenin. *Imperialism, the Highest Stage of Capitalism,* in *The Essential Works of Lenin,* ed. Henry M. Christman (New York: Dover, 1966), 193–194.

28. One can see the parallel here between Joe's authority and that of Delamere in *The Marrow of Tradition* both lack any substantial ground and are purely the product of belief.

29. Monopoly capitalism, because of its emphasis on the ordering center, is thus the most phallic stage of capitalism.

30. Slavoj Žižek, *Looking Awry: An Introduction to Jacques Lacan Through Popular Culture* (Cambridge, MA: MIT Press, 1991), 33.

31. Žižek, *Enjoy Your Symptom*, 94, his emphasis.

32. Joe himself must also believe that he has "something" when he has the phallus. In other words, Joe is not consciously deceiving the town with the illusoriness of his phallic power; he must first deceive himself.

33. For an explanation of the quilting point's ideological function, see Slavoj Žižek, *For they know not what they do: Enjoyment as a political factor* (New York: Verso, 1991), 16–31.

34. Thus, the incessant deconstruction of the center subverts a mode of domination—that of monopoly capitalism—which has already been superseded, or deconstructed, by the subsequent ideology of late capitalism. In *The Culture of Narcissism*, Christopher Lasch constantly upbraids the Left for precisely this— for attacking elements of ideology that are no longer dominant. He says, "Cultural radicalism, posing as a revolutionary threat to the status quo, in reality confines its criticism to values already obsolescent and to patterns of American capitalism that have long ago been superseded" (Christopher Lasch, *The Culture of Narcissism: American Life in An Age of Diminishing Expectations* [New York: Norton, 1979], 114). While Lasch is not incorrect, he does fail to consider the residual power of older "patterns of American capitalism." The very term that Lasch employs—"superseded"—implies that older ideological patterns continue to work alongside dominant ones.

35. Thornton, " 'Goin' on de Muck,' " 267.

36. Thomas Cassidy, "Janie's Rage" The Dog and the Storm in *Their Eyes Were Watching God*," *CLA Journal* 36 (1993): 264.

37. The rabid dog's bite is a moment of transition, in Hegel's terms, from in-itself to for-itself. At this point, Tea Cake's domination of Janie, which has been unconscious, comes to consciousness. If we recognize this continuity in Tea Cake's domination of Janie, it becomes clear Tea Cake's physical abuse is not something exceptional, but symptomatic. This is what John Lowe misses when he laments recent critical attacks on Tea Cake and accuses Tea Cake's detractors of "presentism." Lowe claims, "Readings that insist on applying contemporary standards to texts written in and about a different culture almost sixty years in the past are simply ahistorical presentist interpretations of both literature and culture. It is worth noting that until this line of argument was raised, many critics quite rightly praised this novel as one of the great love stories in our literature; unfortunately, that reading seems to be receding as an important but not definitive detail of the narrative has been interpreted out of context" (Lowe, *Jump at the Sun*, 187). In other words, without this "important but not definitive detail," there would be no ground for seeing domination on the part of Tea Cake. What this argument fails to see is that this domination is far from being limited to this one incident, but pervades the entirety of Tea

Cake and Janie's relationship. In fact, the physical abuse is not even one of the more significant indications of Tea Cake's control over Janie, because it is a moment where his ideological authority breaks down and, as he is forced to exercise his power, his weakness is exposed.

38. Cassidy, "Janie's Rage," 264.

39. For a discussion of Tea Cake's domination of Janie throughout their relationship, see Carla Kaplan, "The Erotics of Talk: 'That Oldest Human Longing' in *Their Eyes Were Watching God*," *American Literature* 67 (1995): 115–142. Kaplan's excellent essay also counters attempts to see *Their Eyes* as a celebration of voice and community. She argues that "the reconciliation of Janie and her community argued for by contemporary critics derives, I think, from our own nostalgia and longing for forms of communal life" (Kaplan, "Erotics," 135).

40. Lasch, *Culture of Narcissim*, xvi.

41. In *The Metastases of Enjoyment*, Žižek points out that this command "Enjoy!" is the precise way in which domination works today: "In post-liberal societies, [. . .] the agency of social repression no longer acts in the guise of an internalized Law or Prohibition that requires renunciation and self-control; instead, it assumes the form of a hypnotic agency that imposes the attitude of 'yielding to temptation'—that is to say, its injunction amounts to a command: 'Enjoy yourself!'" (Slavoj Žižek, *The Metastases of Enjoyment: Six Essays on Woman and Causality* [New York: Verso, 1994], 16).

42. The fact that Tea Cake restores Janie's money through gambling is not an insignificant detail, but one that confirms his mode of subjectivity as that of the pathological narcissist. Unlike Logan Killicks, the devotee of the work ethic, Tea Cake stakes his fundamental belief in chance rather than in work. That the game is dice offers further indication of this. As David Sheppard notes, "Not cards—there would be some skill involved in that—but dice, a game of pure chance" (David Sheppard, "Living by Comparisons: Janie and Her Discontents," *English Language Notes* 30 [1992]: 71).

43. Lasch, *Culture of Narcissism*, 180.

44. Jacques Lacan, *The Seminar of Jacques Lacan, Book I: Freud's Papers on Technique, 1953–1954*, trans. John Forrester (New York: Norton, 1988), 142.

45. Mark Seem, Introduction to *Anti-Oedipus: Capitalism and Schizophrenia*, by Gilles Deleuze and Félix Guattari, trans. Robert Hurley, Mark Seem, and Helen R. Lane (Minneapolis: University of Minnesota Press, 1983), xvi. This question is also present, most famously, in the work of the Frankfurt School. As Adorno and Horkheimer say in *Dialectic of Enlightenment*: "As naturally as the ruled always took the morality imposed upon them more seriously than did the rulers themselves, the deceived masses are today captivated by the myth of success even more than the successful are. Immovably, they insist on the very ideology which enslaves them. The misplaced love of the common people for the wrong that is done them is a greater force than the cunning of the authorities" (Max Horkheimer and Theodor W. Adorno, *Dialectic of Enlightenment*, trans. John Cumming [New York: Continuum, 1991], 133–134).

46. Cassidy, "Janie's Rage," 269.

47. The contemporary explosion of romantic love shows it to be the predominant mode of escaping alienation in late capitalism.

48. This also explains the "teleological" aspect of Hurston's novel. Rather than seeing this as exemplary of a masculinist narrative linearity, we should see Hurston's more Hegelian point: our stories are teleological because we always write them retroactively, because we begin at the end. For a different view of Hurston's narrative, see Margaret Houmans, "Feminist Fictions and Feminist Theories of Narrative," *Narrative* 2 (1994): 3–16.

Chapter Six

1. Roland Barthes, "The Death of the Author," in *Image—Music—Text,* trans. Stephen Heath (New York: Hill and Wang, 1977), 142.

2. In "Signature Event Context" as elsewhere, Derrida emphasizes the ability of writing to make clear the subject's lack of presence: "To write is to produce a mark that will constitute a kind of machine that is in turn productive, that my future disappearance in principle will not prevent from functioning and from yielding, and yielding itself to, reading and rewriting" (Jacques Derrida, "Signature, Event, Context," in *Margins of Philosophy,* trans. Alan Bass [Chicago: University of Chicago Press, 1982], 316).

3. Jacques Derrida, *Of Grammatology,* trans. Gayatri Chakravorty Spivak (Baltimore: Johns Hopkins University Press, 1974), 178. In *Anti-Oedipus,* Deleuze and Guattari conceive of subject as secondary to the machine, rather than to writing (but, as the previous note makes clear, writing is itself a machine for Derrida): "the subject [is] produced as a residium alongside the machine, as an appendix, or as a spare part adjacent to the machine" (Gilles Deleuze and Félix Guattari, *Anti-Oedipus: Capitalism and Schizophrenia,* trans. Robert Hurley, Mark Seem, and H. R. Lane [Minneapolis: University of Minnesota Press, 1983], 20). It is perhaps this shared critique of the subject which, despite vast differences among them, most clearly links the thinkers that are commonly labeled "poststructuralist."

4. Michel Foucault, *The Order of Things: An Archaeology of the Human Sciences* (New York: Random House, 1994), 342.

5. Foucault himself, in his later work, began to reevaluate his dismissal of the subject, announced so definitively in *The Order of Things.* In the return to Antiquity in volumes two and three of *The History of Sexuality (The Use of Pleasure* and *The Care of the Self)*, Foucault begins to develop a notion of subject in terms of what he calls an "aesthetics of existence." Though this does not represent a return to the Cartesian subject, it does suggest that "subject" does not always coincide with "subjection"; subject can, in fact, be a source of liberation, or a style of living. Foucault comes to this transformation in his thought through his history of the Greece of Antiquity. What attracts Foucault to the Greeks is the idea that subject can have agency without the dimension of subjection to the law. In this way, though he begins to embrace an idea of subject

as agent, Foucault remains a poststructuralist, because he continues to see law as a wholly repressive force, a force *that might be avoided*. Foucault seems implicitly to praise the Greek "aesthetics of existence" for its avoidance of law and its focus on self-mastery instead of universal subjection. What Foucault passes over in silence is the way in which such a nonuniversal ethics requires a relation of exclusivity—a master-slave relationship between those who participate in the "aesthetics of existence" and those whom the masters differentiate themselves from. This is why the universalization of the law is, as Lacan claims, liberatory in the first instance: without a universalizing law there is always and necessarily a master-slave relationship. See also Michel Foucault, "An Aesthetics of Existence" in *Politics, Philosophy, Culture: Interviews and Other Writings, 1977–1984* (New York: Routledge, 1988), 47–53.

6. Paul Smith, *Discerning the Subject* (Minneapolis: University of Minnesota Press, 1988), 72.

7. Judith Butler, for one, sees no necessary connection between the loss of the subject and an inability to theorize agency. In *Gender Trouble,* she states, "Construction is not opposed to agency; it is the necessary scene of agency, the very terms in which agency is articulated and becomes culturally intelligible" (Judith Butler, *Gender Trouble: Feminism and the Subversion of Identity* [New York: Routledge, 1990], 147). However, this claim is tautological, because Butler's idea of agency consists in the *subversion* of identity. For her, "The critical task is [. . .] to locate strategies of subversive repetition enabled by those constructions [of identity], to affirm the local possibilities of intervention through participating in precisely those practices of repetition that constitute identity and, therefore, present the immanent possibility of contesting them" (Butler, 147).

8. Henry Louis Gates Jr., *Loose Canons: Notes on the Culture Wars* (New York: Oxford University Press, 1992), 36.

9. Paul Lauter, *Canons and Contexts* (New York: Oxford University Press, 1991), 157. In *Blindness and Insight,* De Man claims that "the bases for historical knowledge are not empirical facts but written texts, even if these texts masquerade in the guise of wars or revolutions" (Paul de Man, *Blindness and Insight: Essays in the Rhetoric of Contemporary Criticism,* 2nd ed. [Minneapolis: University of Minnesota Press, 1983], 165).

10. In *Essentially Speaking,* Fuss argues that "constructionism (the position that differences are constructed, not innate) really operates as a more sophisticated form of essentialism. The bar between essentialism and constructionism is by no means as solid and unassailable as advocates of both sides assume it to be" (Diana Fuss, *Essentially Speaking: Feminism, Nature, and Difference* [New York: Routledge, 1989], xii). Later, she defends Luce Irigaray's essentializing of "woman": "To claim that 'we are women from the start' has this advantage— a political advantage perhaps pre-eminently—that a woman will never be a woman solely in masculine terms, never be wholly and permanently annihilated in a masculine order" (Fuss, *Essentially Speaking,* 61). The problem with this claim is that the symbolic identity "women" which becomes the source of the "we" is always already figured in "masculine terms," which is why Fuss's strategic use of

essentialism falls back within the poststructuralist critique of identity, even as it attempts to acknowledge it.

11. Ernesto Laclau and Chantal Mouffe, *Hegemony and Socialist Strategy* (London: Verso, 1985), 115.

12. Ibid., 166–167, their emphasis.

13. Hence, the absence of any significant reference to the Frankfurt School— Herbert Marcuse is mentioned once (derisively) in passing—in a work of which half is devoted to a history of important developments in Marxist thought, is not surprising; neither is the near-absence of the term "ideology." Though Laclau and Mouffe rightly apprehend the open and contingent nature of political action, they tend to deemphasize the way in which ideology shapes symbolic identities, the way in which ideology *is* the discourse that produces narratives of subject position. This is, of course, the fundamental insight of the Frankfurt School. In Laclau's later work, he gives voice to his objection to the Frankfurt School: "Contrary to the assumptions of the thinkers of the Frankfurt School, the decline of the 'major actors,' such as the working class of classical socialism, has not led to a decrease in social struggles or the predominance of a one-dimensional man, but to a proliferation of new antagonisms" (Ernesto Laclau, *New Reflections on the Revolution of Our Time* [London: Verso, 1990], 214). Here again, because he refuses any notion of ideology, Laclau misses the possibility that a "proliferation of new antagonisms" can coexist with "the predominance of a one-dimensional man."

14. According to Herbert Marcuse, this ability to assimilate "antagonistic contents" without transformation marks the victory of "one-dimensional society," in which "the new totalitarianism manifests itself precisely in a harmonizing pluralism, where the most contradictory works and truths peacefully co-exist in indifference" (Herbert Marcuse, *One-Dimensional Man* [Boston: Beacon Press, 1964], 61).

15. The sustained project of Deleuze and Guattari in *Anti-Oedipus* and later works is to break definitively from this circle of reappropriation. While such a break clearly seems liberating, it would entail the loss of reality's ontological consistency. Without the repressiveness of reappropriation, there is nothing. This is the point behind Lacan's reworking of Dostoyevsky in his *Seminar II:* "If God doesn't exist, then nothing at all is permitted any longer" (Jacques Lacan, *The Seminar of Jacques Lacan, Book II: The Ego in Freud's Theory and in the Technique of Psychoanalysis, 1954–1955,* trans. Sylvana Tomaselli [New York: Norton: 1988], 128). God, here, is that signifier which reappropriates, which quilts all other signifiers and arrests their slippage.

Index

Made in the USA
Lexington, KY
14 March 2016